MEDIA ARCHITECTURE COMPENDIUM VOL. 2
CONCEPTS,
METHODS,
PRACTICE

Joel Fredericks

Glenda Amayo Caldwell

Martin Tomitsch

M. Hank Haeusler

Dave Colangelo

Martijn de Waal

Ava Fatah gen. Schieck

Marcus Foth

Luke Hespanhol

Marius Hoggenmüller

Gernot Tscherteu

avedition

Contents

6	Foreword
8	Preface

10	Concepts

12	Buildings as Screens
16	Networked Space
20	The City as Software
24	Activating Public Places
28	Collaborative City-making
32	Urban Commons
36	Autonomous Agents
40	More-than-human Futures

44	Methods

46	Urban Probes
48	Middle-out Workshops
50	Actor Mapping
52	Intermediation Practices
54	Annotated Portfolios
56	Digital Storytelling
58	Virtual Urban Prototyping
60	Spatial Prototyping
62	Creating Interest
64	Exploring Social Impact

66	Practice

68	Animated Architecture
70	Changi Airport's Terminal 4 'Theatre of Experience'
74	Kipnes Lantern
78	MUURmelaar
82	DAZZLE	San Diego International Airport
86	The Digital Bricks
90	Window into the Seas

94	Money Architecture
96	Hyundai Pavilion Interactive Water Installation
100	Firefly
104	Terrell Place

108	More-than-human Architcture
110	Aukio
114	GROW
118	Touching Night Skies 50°06'44"N 8°40'36"E

122	Participatory Architecture and Infrastructures
124	ARENA
128	Chave do Centro, or 'The Key to Downtown'
132	Digital Calligraffiti
136	ANTopolis
140	Citizen Dialog Kit
144	SP_Urban Arte Conecta

148		Spatial Media Art
	150	Halo
	154	Merck Light Cloud
	158	Where Do We Go From Here?
	162	LEVENSLICHT
	166	Variegation Index
	170	Wervel [Turmoil]
174		Future Trends and Prototypes
	176	SMOG FREE PROJECT
	180	One Shenzen Bay
	184	Archive Dreaming
	188	Novartis Pavillon
	192	Uptown Underground
	196	Woodie
200		Authors
204		Imprint

Foreword

Media architecture is about exploring ways in which we can use technology to rethink how spaces are utilised. In my practice, I am particularly interested in creating data-driven interventions that make the invisible visible in cities. To that end, media architecture is a confluence of social, technological, cultural and environmental concerns and perspectives. At Jason Bruges Studio we as practitioners in the field of media architecture strongly believe that to reimagine our cities in an age of global disruption requires this kind of transdisciplinary thinking. Media architecture is no longer about simply illuminating the physical form of buildings. As media architecture practitioners, we need to ask ourselves questions, such as who benefits from and who is impacted by an urban intervention? In our work we achieve this through operating in the hybrid space between art, architecture and technology.

To illustrate these ideas and to exemplify how we specifically use data in media architecture projects, I will expand on some examples from my practice. Brutalist Tapestry (2018) was an experimental triptych that temporarily replaced the cladding within Beech Street, a tunnel that runs underneath a section of the Barbican Estate in the City of London, with a physical pixel system. The system was programmed to reveal patterns activated by data linked to local cultural activity. The aim of the project was to transform the physical space as well as the perception of people passing through the space. The content displayed on the physical pixel system highlights the cultural significance and potential generated by the cultural institutions that surround the site.

In an earlier project, Thames Pulse (2017), located at Sea Containers House, a mixed-use building which borders the River Thames in London, we used data to visualise the condition of the river in real time. The data was collected and made available by Thames21, a local charity that provides daily water quality readings, and influences the animation displayed on the facade of the building. In addition to making the invisible in the city visible, the project had a strong environmental message and gave a voice to the charity.

While there is still a long way to go, we see the importance of nature in urban settings, and this has influenced our practice. We like to draw attention to the natural world in spaces that are traditionally devoid of it. Variegation Index (2019) represents this approach as it responds to photosynthesis readings from living plants. The artwork uses a specialised camera to look at the changing levels of chlorophyll in the leaves of nearby plants and relays this information across a cascading cellular canvas, amplifying the presence of nature in this way.

Environmental discussions are always embedded within a social and cultural setting. In order to have a productive discourse, we need to acknowledge and consider this in media architecture projects. In our practice, we consider urban architecture as a stage, the public as performers and the design practice as a choreographer or set designer. Shadow Wall (2019) exemplifies this kind of thinking as a monochromatic media artwork located in a pedestrian underpass. The installation functions as a disrupter, or a frame, that reveals people's silhouettes on the surface of the underpass to create an interactive urban canvas. The intention is to bring things into focus and people into the present moment to enjoy their physical relationship with the space.

As mentioned above, we see the city as a stage, and the stage is, of course, not a blank space. Urban data requires context; interesting data might be found in the most difficult spaces, but we are interested in the challenges they provide for our work. Platform 5 (2011) gives the impression people are arriving and waiting for trains on a redundant platform. Set in the context of the redevelopment of the Sunderland train station, on the Durham Coast Line in the UK, we created an LED glass block wall to conceal the unused platform. The huge low-resolution video matrix displayed a generative algorithm displaying various characters interacting with each other and waiting for trains to arrive, which were influenced by the arrival and departure of the trains. The installation features 35 local volunteers who were filmed as if they were waiting for the train. Their movements were digitally deconstructed and reassembled to create the animated characters that appeared on the installation.

The growth of human-generated data in cities means we have the opportunity to increase self-awareness and create playful interference on everyday journeys. This can inspire new thoughts and behaviours that may have a positive influence on our daily actions. It creates a huge opportunity for the field of media architecture. When environmental data inputs are added, it takes the authorship of the content away from the viewer, and the artwork starts to have a life of its own. It becomes a living system, and, in my opinion, it is this aspect of growth, regeneration and renewal that can enhance wellbeing.

For me, media architecture is about hacking an environment. It's about introducing bespoke technologies that illuminate unseen systems and allowing these systems to orchestrate the work so you can begin a conversation about them. This is where this book comes into play. It provides the concepts, methods and examples from practice to spark conversations and bring ideas to life. It's about how we can collectively shift the future of our cities.

Jason Bruges
Founder of Jason Bruges Studio
London, February, 2023

Preface

This is the fourth instalment of the media architecture book series published by the Media Architecture Institute and av edition. The first book, *Media Facades*, published in 2009, explored the integration of digital media into the physical fabric of buildings as an emerging phenomenon. Discussing the history, technology and content of media facades, it set out a foundation for the field. Projects included in the book were large-scale and mostly covering entire building facades.

The second book, *New Media Facades*, published in 2012, presented a global survey of media facade projects. It documented trends that were unique to geographical areas, linking them to cultural factors. Many of the featured projects again spanned entire building facades, but there were also projects of a smaller scale and more spatial in their form. We especially observed this as an emerging trend in Europe at the time. The book also presented new technologies, including green media facades and complex curved facades to enable new typological forms.

The third book, *Media Architecture Compendium*, published in 2017, acknowledged that the field had started to move from large-scale facades towards interventions at different scales, permeating all parts of urban life. The featured projects were the nominees presented at the Media Architecture Biennale 2014 in Aarhus, Denmark, and 2016 in Sydney, Australia. To explore this new role of media architecture in an age of smart cities, we invited academic scholars and industry experts from our global network to contribute articles covering definitions, theories, governance and more.

Much has changed since 2017. The world's cities have been shaken by a global pandemic and extreme weather events. The field of media architecture has responded to these developments, looking for ways to go beyond the technological, cultural and social layers that defined media architecture practice and research in the past. In recognition of this shift, the 2020 Media Architecture Awards introduced a new category for more-than-human architecture. At the same time, technological advancements have brought about a robotic revolution, enabling the implementation of autonomous urban infrastructures.

When we started working on this second compendium, we realised that we had both an opportunity and an obligation to capture the complex network of constituents that define the role of digital media in cities today and in the future. Realising that this was not a task we were able to tackle alone, we invited experts from our international network to join us as co-authors. While each of the authors contributed their expertise to specific chapters, we worked closely together throughout the process to give the book a coherent narrative.

By bringing eleven authors together, we were able to cover a diverse range of perspectives, which is reflected in the 'Concepts' section of the book. Collectively, the authors also brought to the book decades of experience in using and studying specific methods that promote media architecture thinking. The book is the first to document these methods, making them available for others to use in their research, teaching and projects. The 'Methods' section of the book outlines the value each method provides and when and where it can be applied. The practical steps for how to use each method are provided via the book's companion website (mac2.mediaarchitecture.org). The 'Practice' section of the book documents the 2018 and 2020 Media Architecture Award nominees and serves as inspiration for future work in the field.

Like each of the previous books in the media architecture series, this compendium takes an entirely reimagined approach in terms of how it presents and contributes to knowledge in the field. We hope the book inspires you to reimagine the role of media architecture thinking in your work and how digital media can be used to meaningfully and responsibly shape life in future cities.

Joel Fredericks
Glenda Amayo Caldwell
Martin Tomitsch
M. Hank Haeusler

Sydney and Brisbane,
February, 2023

CONCEPTS

Media architecture explores the design and development of interactive and responsive environments, where digital media and physical space interact innovatively. This section of the book delves into the central concepts that are shaping the field, presenting the insights and perspectives of leading scholars. From the impact of technology on our experience of public space to imaginative scenarios for our future cities, these concepts offer a window into the exciting and ever-evolving practice of media architecture.

From 'Buildings as Screens' to 'More-than-human Futures', this section covers a range of topics that are shaping the future of our built environment. The first two chapters discuss how technology is transforming the way we experience public space and how 'Networked Space' is changing our relationship with the city. The third chapter presents the notion of 'The City as Software' and how this perspective lends itself to generating speculative future scenarios.

The concepts of 'Activating Public Space' and 'Collaborative City-making', documented through chapters four and five, explore the role of media architecture in creating lively, inclusive and participatory public spaces. The sixth chapter proposes 'Urban Commons' as a way for media architecture to support the creation of shared spaces for social and cultural activities. The final two chapters in this section consider the potential impact of 'Autonomous Agents' on the future of our cities and and how media architecture can contribute to 'More-than-human Futures'.

The section provides a comprehensive overview of emerging concepts in media architecture, offering a solid foundation for further exploration and learning. It is intended for those with an interest in the field, including students, researchers, practitioners and professionals, who wish to deepen their understanding of this exciting and rapidly evolving field.

Buildings as Screens

When buildings and screens merge—when media and architecture become intertwined—such as at a drive-in theatre or in a digital screen-filled urban centre like Toronto's Yonge-Dundas Square, it can enable and necessitate the development of new theories, practices and audience experiences. The relocation of cinema into architecture blends the logics of urban space, monumentality and the public sphere with the aesthetics and affordances of digital communication and the moving image. Applying the theories and practices of media studies, and in particular cinema studies, to media architecture can support a deeper understanding of this evolving field and how to work critically and creatively within it. The following sections will expand upon how media architecture can be better understood and evaluated using analytical tools from cinema studies, namely superimposition, montage and apparatus/dispositif, by applying them to a recent case study, the M+ museum in Hong Kong.

Superimposition

According to film theorist Tom Gunning, superimposition is the 'incongruous juxtaposition' of images in film that 'yields an eerie image of the encounter of two ontologically separate worlds'.[1] In film, for example, this might serve the purpose of revealing some internal state, such as an aspect of memory, or connect the action to another space or time. Of course, these superimpositions occur within the physical and conceptual limits of the frame: the diegetic space in cinema. Superimpositions in media architecture, such as projections that present the history of a building on the building itself, can enact these same possibilities while extending the potential for ontological hybridity, narrative and creative expansion.

1 - Gunning, T. (2013). To Scan a Ghost: The Ontology of Mediated Vision. In M. del Pilar Blanco & E. Peeren (Eds.), *The Spectralities Reader: Ghosts and Haunting in Contemporary Cultural Theory* (pp. 207–244). Bloomsbury Academic.

Montage

Typically, montage in film is achieved during editing by combining different shots with one another, cutting, recombining and layering film in order to create relationships between images. Montage in film is primarily diegetic—within the frame. Rarely, if ever, does montage explicitly reference or interact with its frame and that which lies beyond it, where the frame is assumed to be the neutral black edges of a darkened theatre, a television set or, more commonly now, a mobile device.

The nature of montage changes when the moving image leaves standardised formats of presentation and is located on a unique surface. Montage in media architecture is by necessity within the shared frame of an architectural or urban space, such as urban screens, public projections or media facades. When montage occurs in public space, for example, when a large digital display incorporates a video feed of its surroundings, the logic of the monument and the logic of the cinema are combined to expand the dimensions of a site. This fosters greater narrative and associative flexibility between moving images, architecture and people.

Apparatus/Dispositif

The transformation of buildings into screens also exhibits expanded and experimental elements of the cinematic concepts of apparatus and dispositif. In cinema, dispositif is 'a network of relations between a spectator, the representation and the "machinery" that allows the spectator to have access to the representation'.[2] The dispositif of cinema also allows the representation to have access to the spectator: it is the ideological interface that captures and captivates, delivering an audience to a message. Apparatus, on the other hand, is

2 - Albera, F., & Tortajada, M. (Eds.). (2010). *Cinema Beyond Film: Media Epistemology in the Modern Era (Film Culture in Transition)* (2nd ed.). Amsterdam University Press.

a term better used to refer to the technical aspects of this field and encompasses the concrete elements of dispositif. For cinema, the apparatus includes the screen, the projector, the film, the seats and so on, without which the cinema effect does not exist.

When buildings become screens, the apparatus is less clearly defined than for the cinema. It includes elements of the city and the application of media, such as projectors, screens, speakers and various interface elements. This is not to mention the complexities of considering the city itself as an interface, or dispositif/apparatus, with its array of signage, sensors, and social actors and their personal devices that constitute contemporary urban life. Here, Nanna Verhoeff's[3] concept of 'composite dispositif'

3 - Verhoeff, N. (2012). *Mobile Screens: The Visual Regime of Navigation* (p. 212). Amsterdam University Press.

is useful. It describes a state of mediation in which environments of spectatorship, such as the cinema, the city or the interface of a smartphone, overlap and constitute a relational experience. Concretely, this might manifest itself in systems such as Digital Out of Home Advertisement (DOOH) that take into account user demographics based on mobile phone data and serve targeted advertisements on digital screens in public spaces. Taken together, the composite dispositif, wherein media architecture plays an important role, forms the basis for the arrangement of demands, desires, fantasies and speculations for corporations, citizens and the city alike. The following section applies the above cinema and media theories—superimposition, montage and apparatus/dispositif—to an installation on the facade of the M+ museum in Hong Kong.

Cinema+

In 2021, the M+ museum presented one of the most exciting and anticipated sites for innovation and experimentation in media architecture. In collaboration with architects Herzog & de Meuron, Swiss studio iart designed a 110-metre-wide by 65.8-metre-tall LED installation that overlooks the city's harbour. As they note, the installation 'transforms the towering facade into a colossal screen, bringing the museum into visual dialogue with the urban landscape and Hong Kong's dynamic skyline'.[4] It does so by showcasing museum collections and brand messaging, but more importantly, through the display of new artworks specifically commissioned for the space.

4 - iart (2021, November 13). *M+ Museum in Hong Kong Now Open.* iart. https://iart.ch/en/news/medienfassade-mplus-hongkong

One such work that was displayed is Hong Kong media artist Ellen Pau's piece, co-commissioned by Art Basel, entitled *The Shape of Light* (2022). The fourteen-minute video incorporates sign language and other ritualistic gestures to silently, but powerfully, communicate a popular scripture in Buddhism, *The Heart Sutra*, to the city, along with visualisations of natural phenomena like fire, water and light. Pau sees the M+ Facade 'like a lighthouse overlooking the sea, a guardian shining a light to all travellers and homecomers'.[5] Furthermore, Pau notes that her work, timed purposefully to be displayed from 5 pm to 8 pm, through sundown, '... is a juxtaposition of what we can control—the video facade—with what we cannot—the lights from the sky above and the windows of the M+ offices behind the screen, each of the latter signifying the presence of somebody who can appear and leave as they please'.[6] For Pau, *The Shape of Light* purposefully engages with the changes in urban and environmental conditions around it, allowing for relational superimpositions and a rich spatial montage. Viewers and non-viewers alike are incorporated into a diegesis, and thus an apparatus/dispositif that harnesses the city and expands to its scale.

5 - M+ museum (n.d.). *Ellen Pau: The Shape of Light.* M+. Retrieved July 29, 2022 from https://www.mplus.org.hk/en/mplus-facade/the-shape-of-light-ellen-pau

6 - Blair, U., & Pau, E. (2022, May 23). *Healing through the Heart Sutra: Ellen Pau on 'The Shape of Light'.* M+. https://www.mplus.org.hk/en/magazine/an-interview-with-hong-kong-artist-ellen-pau

The M+ Facade, and *The Shape of Light* in particular, presents an interesting mix of cinematic techniques repurposed for the scale and context of the specific built environment of Hong Kong's harbour and skyline: the superimposition of environmental elements, such as light, in the diegesis at a scale that mimics and merges with its surroundings; the subsequent spatial montage that relates

↑ Screening of Ellen Pau's *The Shape of Light* on the M+ Facade, 2022. (Media credit: Lok Cheng. Courtesy of Ellen Pau and M+, Hong Kong.)

the installation to the surrounding architecture, office building inhabitants and flows of boats on the harbour; and the traditional cinematic viewing apparatus of tiered seating at the scale of the city, itself engaged by the placement of the facade at the foot of the harbour and the height of the skyscrapers that surround it. Taken together, these tactics, these relocations of cinema, recentre the audience amidst the unpredictable and largely uncontrollable distractions of urban space. Each of these elements serve to deliver the experience to various actors (viewers, participants and passers-by) through a composite dispositif. They also connect an arts organisation, M+, to the city, creating new and wider publics for encounters with media art. Through media architecture, a unity is inscribed between a collective (the citizens of Hong Kong), a history of media (in this case *The Heart Sutra*) and a place (the city).

Viewing this work through the lens of cinema and media studies situates the work within the rich traditions of their practice. It also highlights how formal and technical elements of media architectural experience design can be superimposed, combined through spatial montage and shaped through an understanding of dispositif/apparatus in order to create spaces that engage collective presence, memory and action.

14   / CONCEPTS / BUILDINGS AS SCREENS

Cities as Cinema, Cinema as Cities

Technologies, tools and practices in the field of media architecture are changing every day, with bigger, brighter and lighter lighting elements and projectors occupying wider swathes of the urban environment. The *building as screen* becomes the *city as cinema*. And just as the main claim of this chapter can be restated as the *screen as building*, one can also see how *city as cinema* can also be reversed into *cinema as city* as evidenced by the development of virtual reality and augmented reality, most notably in the recent push towards the metaverse. When buildings become screens and cities become cinemas (and vice versa) they also bring with them additional possibilities and pitfalls with respect to equity (environmental and social), access, representation and power. The histories and theories of media and communication studies, such as film studies, allow for the situating of media architecture within this lineage, while also providing tools of analysis and production that can lead to critical and creative work in the field.

In addition to this, improvements and developments in associated media forms, such as social media and embedded networked sensors, are undergoing similarly rapid changes. This is evidenced by the increased importance of the Internet of Things (IoT), big data and smart city initiatives, which seek to create networks of sensitive, communicative objects through embedded electronics in cities. These can react to intelligent and highly surveilled observers and objects in order to achieve greater efficiency. Regional variations in technologies, economies, network protocols, social networks, aesthetic preferences, demographics, arts organisations and city planning departments serve to further alter the potentials and pitfalls of media architecture's emerging forms of communication and artistic expression. Finally, as media architecture develops and expands, the causes and concerns to which it may be directed are also increasing. Audiences are continuing to develop the skills and affinities necessary for more meaningful interactions in the hybrid media spaces and narratives engaged by media architecture. As urban media environments grow in size, popularity, diversity and complexity, as buildings become screens and cities become cinemas, the development of theories and practices that account for and merge existing theories and practices of media and communication are vital. Doing so will lead to a deeper understanding of media architecture's critical potential for cities and citizens and its efficacy in building empathy, connection and context across online and offline spaces and cultures through participatory, spatialised narrative.

Networked Space

Over the past decade, there has been a growing awareness of the effect of the spatial layout and its configuration in the construction of patterns of co-presence between people in a space. Fundamentally, what happens locally in any individual space is primarily influenced by the relationships between that space and the network of spaces to which it is connected globally.[1] This matter has become more complex with the presence of media architecture and urban media installations, as they offer new ways to mediate between people in the same space or with others to whom they are connected remotely.

1 - Hillier, B. (1996). *Space is the Machine: a Configurational Theory of Architecture.* Cambridge University Press.

When situating media architecture within the city context, it becomes part of a larger system of networks and infrastructures, physical and digital, which consists of, but is not limited to, humans, living and non-living matter, and platforms as components. Interactions are generated at the threshold between networks of 'media infrastructure',[2] defined as a material network that is organised to disseminate audiovisual digital content in urban public spaces, and of 'spatial infrastructure', defined as an interactively connected set of geographic data, metadata and tools. An important feature of interaction spaces generated through the presence of media architecture and urban installations is that they are defined by the properties of the architectural setting and the space in which they are placed, as well as the properties of the medium itself. Going beyond local interactions, opportunities for hybrid networked infrastructures, physical and digital, which connect places across spatial, geographical and cultural boundaries have grown over the last decade.

2 - Parks, L. (2015). Stuff You Can Kick: Towards a Theory of Media Infrastructures. In P. Svensson & D. T. Goldberg (Eds.), *Between Humanities and the Digital* (1st ed., p. 357). MIT Press.

Whereas the social aspects and media affordances are often considered by interaction designers, relatively little attention has been given to the individual aspects of the place, its spatial network properties and the hybrid spatial experience.[3] While it is well understood how architectural spatial layout and its network properties give rise to movement and patterns of encounter, there has been too little consideration for media infrastructure as a facet of urban design.

Against this backdrop, this chapter explores the effect of urban networks on our mediated experiences: 1) lived primarily at that space and time and generated through the structure of the spatial layout (example one) or 2) hybrid experiences extended to remote places across geographical boundaries (example two). To help examine these effects, a framework is presented, which addresses the combination of physical and digital networks and their effect on emergent local and remote interactions.

3 - Behrens, M., Fatah gen. Schieck, A., Kostopoulou, E., North, S., Motta, W., Ye, L. & Schnädelbach, H. (2013, June). Exploring the Effect of Spatial Layout on Mediated Urban Interactions. In *PerDis '13: Proceedings of the 2nd ACM International Symposium on Pervasive Displays.* Mountain View, United States of America (79–84). Association for Computing Machinery.

From a spatial and physical layout perspective,[4] this framework covers three spatial scales:

> **The micro-scale:** is where embodied interactions provide (intended or unintended) input to the interactive system, and the movement flow and patterns of human presence can be amplified or intensified through the media architecture medium affordance and its materiality.

4 - Afonso, A., & Fatah gen Schieck, A. (2020). Play in the smart city context: exploring interactional, bodily, social and spatial aspects of situated media interfaces. *Behaviour & Information Technology, 39*(6), pp. 656–680.

> **The meso-scale:** refers to encounters around media architecture installations that link to their immediate surroundings, for instance, to the presence of features such as

16 / CONCEPTS

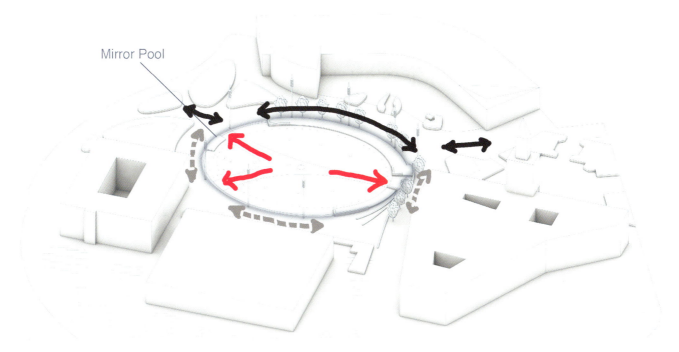

↑ The urban context of the Mirror Pool, and the art installation *Another Life*, with its constantly changing and dynamic behaviour that creates new urban routes over time. (Image adapted from Cannon Ivers 2018—with permission.)

water, greenery or sitting areas. In these encounters people are drawn to engage in different behaviours or interact with other people.

> **The macro-scale:** is when media architecture installations form a focal point linking neighbourhoods and functions from across the globe. This leads to the creation of a high level of pedestrian flow, which in turn influences the intensity of mediated interactions at the location of the installation.

From a digital interaction point of view, a networked media infrastructure creates three distinct interaction zones[3] included in the framework as:

> **Direct interaction zone:** is at the location of the installation which is embodied and defined by the affordances of the media architecture medium itself.

> **Wide interaction zone:** spans to the immediate and extended surroundings of the media architecture installation and is supported by the digital interaction space created by the installation.

> **Networked interaction zone:** is created by the media architecture installation across spatial and temporal boundaries, connecting one or more urban spaces remotely beyond their local space or time.

In the following section, two projects are selected to demonstrate how the framework can be applied for media architecture deployments: 1) City Park, with a standalone media art installation as part of a large-scale regeneration project embedded in the urban spatial network and 2) Screens in the Wild, a digital infrastructure of four networked displays connecting two cities. These projects are not new; however, they are selected as they reveal unique ways of situating media installations and how they relate to the urban setting on three levels locally, globally and remotely. Crucially, both examples are designed as an integral part of the urban setting, on a permanent or long-term basis, and both successfully demonstrated the importance of considering the role of 1) the global spatial network as a

↑ Two display nodes (London), offering mediated experiences, shared in real-time with all four display locations to draw music patterns and express mood.

generator of shared encounters and 2) the digital network as a mediator that potentially intensifies local or remote interactions.

City Park, 2012 – Bradford, United Kingdom

The park forms a focal point, linking together various neighbourhoods with a major transport hub and a commercial district. At its centre, it contains the Mirror Pool, a large interactive media space with a shallow set of pools and *Another Life*, a standalone media art installation with sensors and projections. The park contains two areas of occupation. The first area is a continuous boardwalk and the second is a discrete area consisting of several spots for sitting. The Mirror Pool mediates the urban experience through its interactive and dynamic behaviour and the continuous change in the water levels defined by three pre-programmed modes.

From an urban spatial perspective, the effect of the spatial network is apparent on the three scales[4] and interaction zones of the framework as follows:

> **The micro-scale + direct zone:** the digital components—such as motion sensors and laser projections—tend to take centre stage and drive the urban experience for spectators, following existing temporal rhythms of the site. They also amplify and generate new urban rhythms, therefore enhancing how people experience the installation. People who engage directly with the installation's materiality and behaviour, provide (intended or unintended) input to the interactive system. This in turn creates a dynamic process, slowly evolving over the course of several years with a direct interaction zone.

> **The meso-scale + wide zone:** the Mirror Pool provides two contrasting experiences: 1) a clear and dry causeway, which creates alternative pedestrian routes and 2) central fountains activated in the middle of the causeways, turning these routes into interactive spaces for play. The spatial layout links the pool to its immediate surroundings. Due to the presence of water features, people are drawn to engage in activities or interact with other people, creating rhythms of localised static activities (such as observing, sitting, talking and playing). The level of interaction zone is wide.

> **The macro-scale**: factors that are unique to the central area of Bradford played a crucial role in the design and construction processes of the Mirror Pool. The position of the park in the urban layout gives the area a transient character, creating a place with high levels of pedestrian flow, where the main axis of circulation stretches through the open space to the north.

Screens in the Wild, 2011 – London and Nottingham, United Kingdom

Going beyond urban media installations as a standalone experience, Screens in the Wild represents an exemplar of a media architecture installation with digital infrastructure that supports a hybrid network of spatial and digital configurations. The overall goal of this project was to integrate the content development, placement, local interactive experiences and distributed digital connectivity using video feed on four separate urban displays that connect Nottingham with London. From the urban spatial perspective, the effect of the spatial network can be revealed on the three scales and interaction zones of the framework as follows:

> **The mico-scale + direct + networked zones:** behaviours which appeared on all four display locations were triggered through the affordance of the media architecture medium itself. The level of interaction zone is direct and networked across spatial and temporal boundaries, connecting physical spaces remotely through the networked experience and the use of video feed. A set of digital interactive experiences were designed to mediate interactions, for example, to express mood, share a collection of photos, draw musical patterns with other people or take a photo with friends. Experiences could be shared through real-time exchanges, like online multiplayer action games, or through asynchronous means similar to social networks, such as Twitter.

> **The meso-scale + wide zone:** due to the presence of a community centre, a local library and an art gallery, the installation provided people with encounters with local communities and linked them to the immediate surroundings.

> **The macro-scale**: this analysis indicates a clear relationship between high display visibility of the media architecture installation and the daily flow of pedestrian movement. Despite the fact that the technical properties were identical in all four sites of the installation, site-specific interactions were observed and different from one location to another. The spatial layout in each location affected how people interacted with the installation.

Crucially, the generated rhythms of mediated interactions correlated directly with the movement flow and urban functions at each location. In other words, the position of each display within the global urban layout and its streets network was what determined the degree and intensity of interaction. The project offered locally situated experiences, structured over time, but also remotely connected ones through distributed (synchronous and asynchronous) experiences. This generated a heightened sense of presence locally, determined, to some extent, by the spatial configuration of the city, yet traversing existing spatial boundaries that occasionally amplified or disrupted local experiences.

Situating Media Architecture and the New Digital Turn

Situating media architecture in the networked and increasingly autonomous city raises a question about how people will experience both the urban space and the interaction space, enabled through new advances in computing, sensing and network technologies. We face the challenge of developing strategies for articulating the new public arena and have to take into account the complex system of networks and infrastructures, with its components, humans and living and non-living matter. Its location within the urban grid is fundamental to the understanding of the 'spatial experience' as an integral part of the city.

This chapter extends existing calls by media architecture scholars to consider urban design knowledge in informing the deployment of future forms of media architecture in public space. There is a need for robust approaches as first steps towards understanding how the new, and potentially hybrid, experience can be designed to augment real-world interactions and so address the key question—how to best integrate a radical and potentially disruptive new technology into the urban realm? Key to successful integration is the notion of 'networked space' and the combination of digital, physical and hybrid infrastructures.

In this chapter, a framework is presented to address the urban spatial layout and the 'physical infrastructure' (micro-scale, meso-scale and macro-scale), and the digital interaction space of the 'media infrastructure' (direct zone, wide zone and networked zone). This framework provides mechanisms for future investigations for interaction design researchers, architects, ethnographers, anthropologists, media artists and theorists wanting to explore new emergent space created by media architecture and its network effect.

The City as Software

Applying 'software' as a metaphor to media architecture offers two useful perspectives that are discussed in this chapter. The first perspective is to view the city as an operating system. The second is to think of media architecture interventions as software applications, also referred to as city apps.[1] Indeed, these two perspectives are closely interlinked, as software applications in a traditional sense typically rely on an operating system to run. The notion of operating systems dates back to the early 1980s, with MS-DOS representing one of the first commercially successful and widely adopted operating systems. Today, we have operating systems for smartphones, watches and even TVs. Two key components of an operating system are drivers and the application programming interface (API). Drivers provide access to peripheral hardware components like printers, cameras and microphones. The API enables applications to exchange data and communicate with each other.

1 - Tomitsch, M. (2017). City Apps as Urban Interfaces. In A. Wiethoff & H. Hussmann (Eds.), *Media Architecture: Using Information and Media as Construction Material* (pp. 81–102). De Gruyter Saur.

The API is conceptually quite different to the user interface (UI), which is another key element of software applications. In computing devices, the UI supports the user's interaction with an application. This includes both displaying content (providing output) as well as interactive mechanisms (enabling input). Like software applications, media architecture installations feature a UI to communicate content to passers-by and also, in some cases, to support direct or indirect user interaction. Output most commonly occurs in the form of visual media content (images, videos or animations), for example, displayed on the facade of a building. Input is used in media architecture installations to enable passers-by to either directly or indirectly manipulate the displayed content. Project Blinkenlights was an early media architecture example that included both output and input channels. The project allowed people to upload animations remotely via their desktop computer and to play games on the facade using their mobile phone.

By applying the city as a software perspective, media architecture becomes more than just a canvas for displaying content and enabling people to interact. Rather than just offering a localised media touchpoint, the notion suggests that media architecture is a distributed system, connecting individual city apps through a conceptual operating system. A somewhat simplified manifestation of this concept is the traffic light system used in cities, with individual traffic lights serving as localised touchpoints while being connected through an underlying common infrastructure. However, the city as a software concept does not suggest centralised control, which is often the case with traffic lights. City apps that are conceptually connected might further take different appearances and forms and serve varied purposes.

The City as an Operating System

We can think about the city as an operating system with the city consisting of components that are all connected. Importantly, the metaphor is only used in a conceptual way—this is not a call for developing an actual software-based city operating system. That kind of thinking would be more akin to early smart city approaches, with large information and communication technology providers attempting to sell their city software operating system to city authorities. This approach has been used by companies, for example, to roll out hyperlinked digital information kiosks or to 'program' entire precincts, such as Alphabet Inc.'s Sidewalk Labs development in Toronto.[2] Such an approach is problematic, as it locks cities into a proprietary technology environment.

2 - Mann, M., Mitchell, P., Foth, M., & Anastasiu, I. (2020). #BlockSidewalk to Barcelona: Technological sovereignty and the social license to operate smart cities. *Journal of the Association for Information Science and Technology, 71*(9), 1103–1115.

20 / CONCEPTS

↑ The City Bug Report uses open data provided by the City of Aarhus to bring transparency to the process of civic issues and the progress towards their resolution. (Media credit: Rasmus Steengaard.)

Compared to operating systems developed for computing devices, the city as an operating system is unstructured and less clearly defined. But conceptually this metaphor emphasises the role of the citizen, arguing that they are not only a 'user' but both a consumer and provider of city apps. This shift towards citizen-driven applications in urban environments is further enabled through the open data movement, which has seen city authorities making their data available for anyone to use.

The role of clearly defined drivers, introduced earlier in this chapter as a way to access peripheral hardware, is essential to support this kind of media architecture movement. Beyond drivers, this may also include standardised tools and frameworks. To use smartphones as an example, when Apple released their software development kit (SDK) for the iPhone in 2008, it included tools and frameworks. This made it possible for anyone to develop an app that would instantly be available to millions of people through Apple's app store. Providing an SDK revolutionised the mobile phone industry since it opened smartphones as a platform while also providing a distribution channel.

Similarly, anyone who has the tools and skills can build city apps as software instances of media architecture that use the city as an operating system. City authorities can encourage this through offering appropriate tools and frameworks. This may include providing open data, as mentioned above, or other ways to access city data and infrastructure. For example, the City Bug Report project used open data provided by the City of Aarhus to visualise progress on civic issues raised by citizens.[3] Lodged issues and responses from the city were visualised as an animation on a large-scale LED screen wrapped around the City Hall Tower.

Beyond open data and digital tools, the city as an operating system can include practical frameworks as enablers, such as providing a site and access to power for public

Here we use the notion of the city as an operating system to describe an approach to media architecture: the city provides the infrastructure on top of which city apps are built alongside pre-existing input and output mechanisms. Types of input include urban activities, such as traffic or pedestrian flow, and environmental conditions, such as air quality, temperature and light. Forms of output include surfaces, such as the street or building facades, and urban furniture, such as benches and street lamps.

3 - Korsgaard, H., & Brynskov, M. (2014, November). City Bug Report: Urban prototyping as participatory process and practice. In *MAB '14: Proceedings of the 2nd Media Architecture Biennale Conference: World Cities*. MAB '14: Media Architecture Biennale 2014, Aarhus, Denmark (pp. 21–29). The Association for Computing Machinery.

installations exhibited as part of urban light festivals. For instance, Sydney hosts an annual festival, Vivid Sydney, which features urban light installations from small-scale interventions like the chalk-drawing robot Woodie (p. 196) to activating high-rise buildings. Conceptually, each of these interventions is part of a larger (in this case curated) experience. The inputs provided through the operating system include the moment when all interventions come to life each evening, the movement of crowds and individuals through space, the urban fabric of the spatial environment and so on.

City Applications

Similar to the way software applications run on top of an operating system, media architecture installations can be considered applications running on top of the city as an operating system. These city apps can serve a range of purposes, from making data available to citizens when and where needed to creative placemaking—as demonstrated by the Vivid Sydney light installations mentioned above. An example of a more utilitarian application of media architecture that has already found its way into many cities is the use of digital screens at transport hubs to display upcoming services.

Here the use of the API introduced earlier in the chapter can be a useful vehicle to enable new forms of media architecture. APIs enable applications to connect and communicate with each other. This has been used in cities in China to synchronise the media facades of an entire skyline of high-rise buildings. But the API also enables data exchange across different kinds of applications, such as connecting web-based applications with media architecture installations. An example is the In The Air, Tonight project developed for a media facade in Toronto. The project displayed animations that changed every time someone posted on Twitter using the hashtag #homelessness, which was enabled through connecting the installation with Twitter via an API.

↑ The In The Air, Tonight media facade installation conceptually represents a city app that visualises social media interactions. (Media credit: Public Visualization Studio)

A key element of media architecture is its multidisciplinary approach to city-making, bringing together architectural, societal, cultural and technological thinking. Specifically, the technological layer makes it possible not only to display digital content but to sense, process and visualise data. This characteristic distinguishes the design of city apps from traditional urban design. In that sense, a park bench is not a city app unless its function is augmented through a technology layer. Interfaces that combine digital technology and physical elements in an urban environment, such as traffic light push buttons for pedestrians, can be considered city apps.

This perspective of media architecture as applications can also lead to new opportunities for media architecture interventions. By viewing existing urban artefacts through this lens, it is possible to enhance or transform experiences, like turning a bench into a playful social interaction.[4] Or, returning to the traffic light example, a media architecture

4 - Grönvall, E., Kinch, S., Petersen, M. G., & Rasmussen, M. K. (2014, April). Causing commotion with a shape-changing bench: experiencing shape-changing interfaces in use. In *Proceedings of the SIGCHI Conference on Human Factors in Computing Systems* (pp. 2559–2568)

perspective can offer additional social and cultural perspectives, for instance, enabling people to play Pong with someone across the road while waiting for the crossing signal or adding a political statement by displaying same-sex pedestrian lights.

Ultimately, like any useful software application, media architecture interventions should aim to improve the urban experience, to better inform people and to help citizens make better decisions and use of their cities. Interventions should start from a specific situation or problem rather than being driven by a particular technology.

The Future of the City as a Software

The concept of the city as a software offers a number of opportunities for future media architecture developments and the designers, manufacturers and sponsors of media architecture interventions.

First, it establishes a foundation for creating digital twins through representing the operating system aspects and the individual applications as digital counterparts. These kinds of digital twins can be used to visualise input from real sensors and support agent-based simulations, for example, to simulate occupancy patterns.[5] Mapping out the components of a conceptual city operating system can facilitate and generate new insights for how to create such digital twins. At the same time, media architecture can be used to make digital twins more accessible to citizens through localised interventions.

5 - Grübel, J., Gath-Morad, M., Aguilar, L., Thrash, T., Sumner, R. W., Hölscher, C., & Schinazi, V. (2021). Fused Twins: A Cognitive Approach to Augmented Reality Media Architecture. In *Proceedings of the Media Architecture Biennale 2020* (pp. 215–220)

Second, by considering media architecture interventions as a distributed software system, it is possible to more systematically map out and generate orchestrated experiences. For example, as mentioned earlier, some cities in China have experimented with coordinating media displayed across several buildings. As another example, Times Square, New York displays synchronised artwork across its urban screen ecology, referred to as the Midnight Moment.

Third, it is possible to map other elements of conventional software applications to media architecture, beyond notions of output and input. This could include broader concerns, such as ethics and politics (also discussed in the literature through the notion of 'platform urbanism'), and emerging approaches, such as artificial intelligence, autonomous agents and urban robots—a topic that is further explored later in this book. How these concerns could shape future media architecture will provide promising avenues for research and design explorations.

Fourth, the notion of the city as a software lends itself to generating speculative future scenarios, for example, in the form of short stories that describe one or multiple mediated futures using scenario planning or other futuring methods. For example, the short story *Folding Beijing*[6] explores a future in which Beijing's population is divided into three classes sharing the same urban surface in 48-hour cycles.

6 - Jingfang, H. (2015). Folding Beijing. trans. Ken Liu, *Uncanny Magazine*, 2.

The story illustrates how media and kinetic architectural systems are used to fold living structures. Such speculative scenarios can use new developments in the software world as a starting point, bringing them into the city context. For example, the rise of the metaverse and distributed ledgers provides new opportunities for hybrid media architecture that stretches across physical and digital boundaries.

The images of flickering media facades lighting up the cityscape in the dystopian future of the movie *Blade Runner* are often cited as inspiration for urban media facades. The city as a software concept has the power to generate future scenarios in which media experiences are distributed and orchestrated across the city, transforming and supporting urban life in meaningful ways. It shifts the focus from the hard aspects (the hardware and physical components) to the soft elements in media architecture—the people, their behavioural patterns, urban activities and experiences.

Parts of this chapter were originally published in Tomitsch, M. (2017) Making Cities Smarter: Designing Interactive Urban Applications. JOVIS Verlag GmbH.

Activating Public Places

What Do We Mean by 'Active' and 'Public' Spaces?

Public spaces constitute fundamental elements of city life, the connective tissue that turns otherwise dispersed amalgamations of people and buildings into a whole greater than the sum of its parts. They are generally understood to be spaces that are not only physically but also culturally and socially accessible to all inhabitants of a city. That is, spaces that do not privilege a range of demographics or cultural activities over others and, therefore, encourage shared occupation by diverse individuals and groups who might not have any particular 'parochial' reason to congregate, such as family, work or leisure. An urban space feels *public* when it is perceived as simultaneously belonging to all citizens and no one in particular. On the one hand, this presupposes that public spaces are felt as safe, inviting and welcoming. On the other hand, especially in many of today's hyperdiverse cities, there is frequently a degree of friction and contestation involved, as those spaces continually invite questions of who has the 'right to the city'. A public space feels *active* when it enacts this right for citizens, offering them opportunities to comfortably perform, in full visibility of others, a range of desired activities they otherwise might not.

Clearly, not all shared urban spaces can qualify as truly public or active. The field of 'placemaking' encompasses a range of approaches aimed at developing otherwise nondescript locations into active public spaces, imbued with their own identities and capable of nurturing collective memories by promoting shared experiences in situ. Those approaches may vary from site-specific improvements, such as reclaiming street space for pedestrians, to community-building activities like urban gardening or collective play, to the higher-level curation of cultural programs associated with the precinct, including public events, live music, festivals, markets or public art. They may include activities initiated from the bottom-up, top-down or a combination of both, and may or may not include digital technologies. The term 'digital placemaking', accordingly, has been used for over a decade to describe types of urban interventions resorting to digital media and technologies to enact placemaking efforts.

Interfaces and Strategies

Media architecture activates the built environment through a combination of interfaces and strategies. Interfaces are commonly presented through screens, projections, public lighting, sound, computer vision, motion sensors, QR codes and smartphones, with emerging technologies like augmented reality, robotics and artificial intelligence rapidly gaining terrain. Interfaces provide the means for citizens to engage with people, services and other elements in the built environment, including city apps, which were introduced in the previous chapter. Strategies include, among others, the design of responsive or interactive environments that promote playfulness, animated public art, city data visualisation, digital storytelling and integration with social media. Over the years, combinations of interfaces and strategies have produced multiple examples of public space activations in the form of temporary light installations, public festivals, large-scale projection mapping, augmented reality art trails, screens or locative media telling stories about the community, animated architecture and many others. Key objectives may include: unlocking the city for citizens; creating open-ended venues for spontaneous public appropriation; increasing pedestrian traffic, which may in turn lead to higher levels of patronage to local commercial establishments as well as greater safety through passive surveillance; and subverting the assumed identity of a precinct by offering citizens different perspectives about the kinds of activities they are allowed to perform in it. These interventions shape the perception of public spaces as being alive, open in the dual sense of 'inviting' and 'subject to continual debate' and a special destination within the city.

Reactivating Degraded Spaces
Activations can work even with very well-established public spaces, for example, New York's Times Square. Despite existing as one of the most prominent public spaces in the city for over 100 years, Times Square has often been perceived as gritty and dangerous. Through the decades, its well-known electronic public signage and numerous billboards have become synonymous with wild capitalism and a space sold out to advertisement and private interests, rather than the welfare of the public. In 2012, however, following various revitalisation efforts and occasional experimentation with showing digital arts on the public displays, a new program was launched: Midnight Moment, synchronising six of Times Square's large screens to simultaneously display media art nightly from 11:57 pm to midnight. The program signalled to the public that it could be worth coming to the site late at night to witness its transformation into an open-air gallery—fleeting enough to be special, yet regular enough to become a reliable urban ritual. Over the following decade, Midnight Moment expanded to over 90 billboards in the district and significantly contributed to the renewed identity of Times Square as a safe and refined cultural destination.

A related approach was adopted at Vale do Anhangabaú, an old public space in downtown São Paulo, Brazil. Like Times Square, it is a heritage boulevard, traditionally used as a stage for public gatherings and civic demonstrations. Also like Times Square, it had over many decades experienced decline, high rates of crime and turned into an undesirable destination, particularly in the evenings. In 2019, the local municipality announced plans to reactivate the area, in partnership with the private sector, through physical renovation and establishment of a new cultural, educational and recreational program. The aim was to boost visits by 10,000 people each week, with direct benefits to the local economy. Eventually launched in 2021, the new program included activities such as Mostra Play,

↑ Dance-O-Mat, created by the design collective Gap Filler.

sponsored by Meta and produced by Verve Cultural, a local company specialising in digital urban activations. The event involved a range of local digital artists, who created playful content for a pop-up urban screen installed in the precinct. Given its timing, the project became meaningful, not only as a step towards reactivating Vale do Anhangabaú specifically but also as an incentive for citizens of São Paulo to return to the streets—and to interact with each other—in the wake of the COVID-19 lockdowns.

Healing Collective Trauma
The use of media architecture to activate public spaces after periods of collective grief can also be illustrated by Dance-O-Mat, created by the design collective Gap Filler in Christchurch, New Zealand, in the aftermath of the massive earthquake that destroyed much of the city centre in 2011. With many of the previously existing commercial blocks suddenly turned into empty public spaces or parking lots, grassroots groups like Gap Filler started to experiment with low-cost interventions that could lend new narratives to the area, bringing people together and helping them to heal while also, simultaneously, healing the city itself. Dance-O-Mat consisted of a quadrilateral truss structure with speakers mounted to its corners and a disco ball hanging from

↑ Multi-Arts Pavilion by Lake Macquarie City Council.

the centre, thus delimiting an impromptu dance floor. At one side, an old washing machine hacked with electronics functioned as a jukebox: by inserting coins into a slot, people could temporarily take over the space, playing sounds from their smartphones directly into the speakers. A blackboard and chalk near the 'jukebox' explained how the contraption worked and allowed people to leave names, messages or playlists for others to see. While very simple, Dance-O-Mat soon became very popular, attracting many residents and tourists to a street corner otherwise completely empty. Though it was conceived as an urban hack, its popularity and emotional value to citizens have ensured its longevity: despite subsequently changing locations, Dance-O-Mat remains active in Christchurch to this day, embodying the city's reconstruction and reactivation.

Curating New Space Identities

Activating an otherwise empty space with media architecture was also the strategy adopted by Lake Macquarie City Council, in the Hunter Region of New South Wales, Australia, when planning their new cultural venue: the Multi-Arts Pavilion (MAP mima, where *mima* is a local Awabakal word meaning 'cause to stay'), launched in 2021. A hi-tech gallery for contemporary and experimental art, MAP mima's physical architecture is itself highly flexible, allowing the building to be used for exhibitions, theatre, music concerts and public events. The new venue was placed at an existing public park, popular during the day, yet dark and underused at night. As a strategy to turn the new gallery into an inviting landmark at all times, the Council surrounded the physical building with colourful wash lights, projections, light artworks, responsive audio installations and an interactive lighting system hanging from the catenary structure over the paved promenade leading to the building. The Catenary, designed by Luke Hespanhol, is active nightly for a few hours from sunset and allows visitors to interact with it via a website, creating different kinds of personalised light effects. Stickers installed on the floor display a QR code for visitors to scan and load the website on their smartphones. When not interacted with, the system displays animated patterns, thus conveying that the public space around the venue is open—even though the gallery itself only opens at daytime. Since its launch, the precinct has served as a stage for various community events and encouraged pedestrians and bike riders to regularly visit the space at night. The Council has also observed spontaneous citizen-led pop-up activities, such as groups of skaters gathering weekly under the lights, bringing their own Bluetooth-enabled speakers to further customise the public space's atmosphere.

Benefits and Caveats

These projects demonstrate the value of media architecture for activating public spaces. They illustrate how open and active public spaces are essential to liveable, sustainable and socially cohesive cities, by essentially entailing a positive level of 'friction' between different demographic and cultural groups, which get the chance to see and interact with each other as different-yet-equal members of society. This is particularly important given the dynamics of contemporary digital online life, where social media and recommender systems tend to approximate and reinforce identification between like-minded people who already think similarly, clustering them along social classes, profession, religion, sexual preferences or political values. In that sense, activating urban public spaces works as an antidote to social media fragmentation into so-called 'filter bubbles', by reuniting citizens face-to-face and creating narratives for a city based on equality, tolerance, mutual awareness and respect. By exposing the diversity within a society, they help to advance conversations towards mitigating conflicts, promoting cross-cultural awareness and identifying issues across sectors of society, around which collaborations might emerge. By welcoming citizens, activated spaces prompt a sense of place and belonging, promoting feelings of co-ownership and accountability towards the city.

Given that media architecture operates predominantly in urban public areas, understanding its impact is paramount. While they hold a strong potential for activating public spaces, as demonstrated by the examples above, media architecture interventions do not always support that end. For example, very large media facades may push people away from a precinct, forcing them to areas sufficiently far removed to allow them to properly visualise the digital content, thus creating spaces devoid of social activities immediately around the facade. Other times, the explicit intent of the media architecture intervention is to *not* activate a precinct, for example, where digital media is deployed at areas of high pedestrian traffic, with the goal of aiding frictionless navigation through the city and discouraging people from gathering and 'bumping' into each other. Because of their inherent eye-catching nature and potential to induce curiosity, some forms of media architecture can even activate public spaces inadvertently. Understanding that some public spaces should be activated into becoming destinations, while others must be toned down to function as thoroughfares, is a key skill when designing and deploying media architecture. Just as important as avoiding media architecture misuse, is to avoid its overuse: future contributions should ensure representation, accessibility and equity, while also considering environmental impact. While a powerful tool, media architecture is just one among many approaches for activating public spaces. Its use should, therefore, be balanced against other factors such as cost, impact of light levels on urban wildlife, ability of all citizens to understand and use the technology and to what degree the added urban media integrates with the pre-existing built environment. Whether a public space should be activated, how it should be achieved and whether media architecture should be part of the solution are all questions that ought to be addressed in tandem when designing better places, cities and communities.

Collaborative City-making

Collaborative city-making is the process of fostering relationships between individuals, governments, organisations and the built environment, both within and outside local communities for the purpose of creating better public spaces. Media architecture within the context of collaborative city-making can play a number of significant roles to inform decision-making by a diverse range of actors for the design, development and deployment of digital and physical infrastructure across cities and regional areas.

Cities have a deep history of culture, customs and social interactions that are juxtaposed with policies, laws and social conventions. If we looked at things more closely, we would observe that cities are forever evolving and adapting as a result of contemporary influences, social and cultural awareness, environmental impacts, political ideology and smart city infrastructure. From these glimpses, we could learn from past experiences and mistakes and instead forge a future that values local knowledge and expertise. Community engagement, which is central to collaborative city-making, has been widely practised in the design and development of infrastructure deployed within interior and exterior environments. The general intention of community engagement is to inform local communities about proposed projects and seek their comments through channels, such as information sessions, online platforms and official documents. On the one hand, this approach can produce outcomes based on the feedback received by local communities. On the other hand, the actual needs and wants expressed by people can be ignored by the objectives of top-down decision-makers. Community engagement within city-making has a history of being tokenistic and reduced to 'engagement theatre', that is, simply ticking a box to meet the legislative requirements to inform people about proposed developments—whether they like it or not. This has inspired many grassroots activism movements around the world to take matters into their own hands and drive bottom-up approaches to city-making. By applying this approach, local communities have been empowered to voice their discontent, show power in numbers and ultimately stand up to top-down decision-makers.

Collaborative city-making works on the ethos of drawing on the collective knowledge and input from both top-down and bottom-up actors, allowing them to meet in the middle and work outwardly together. When developing collaborative city-making strategies, three points should be considered:

> Is city-making done *to* people (i.e. top-down)?
> Is city-making done *by* the people (i.e. bottom-up)?
> Should city-making be something done *with* people (i.e. middle-out)?

Middle-out Design to Inform Collaborative City-making

Middle-out design is an approach that can facilitate greater levels of collaboration and inclusion with a diverse range of actors for city-making.[1] The objective is to draw on the collective knowledge of top-down and bottom-up actors to meet somewhere in the middle and actively work outwards together as a representative coalition. The coalition provides a unique opportunity to foster the knowledge, skills and creativity of its members to help address the needs, wants and aspirations of people in the city-making process. The concept of 'middle-out' has been used in a variety of industry and research settings, such as computing, engineering, biochemistry, social sciences and urban interaction design to better engage with a variety of people and to enhance decision-making.

1 - Fredericks, J., Caldwell, G. A., & Tomitsch, M. (2016, November). Middle-out design: collaborative community engagement in urban HCI. In *OzCHI '16: Proceedings of the 28th Australian Conference on Computer-Human Interaction.* Launceston, Tasmania (pp. 200–204). Association for Computing Machinery.

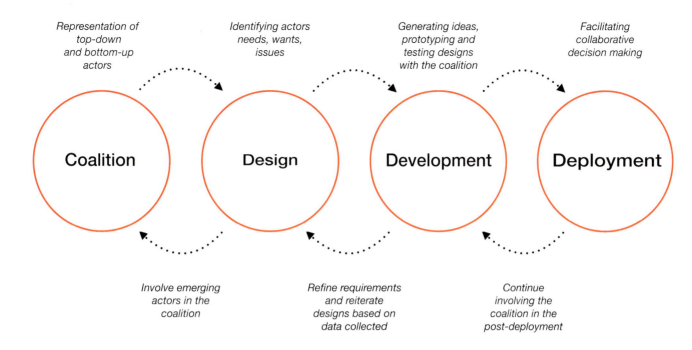

↑ Middle-out Design Framework for collaborative city-making. (Media credit: Joel Fredericks.)

Similar to the Design Council UK framework for innovation,[2] the Middle-out Design Framework puts people first by understanding their needs, strengths and aspirations, and encouraging people to co-create and be inspired by each other.

2 - Design Council (2011). *Design for Innovation*. Design Council, London.

The framework consists of four stages: coalition, design, development and deployment. The stages build on each other, which allows the actors involved to progress through the city-making process. The four stages operate as follows:

1. **Coalition** – The first stage is to identify people that will form part of the coalition, which incorporates three roles: (1) top-down actors, for example, representatives from government agencies, international organisations and private enterprise; (2) bottom-up actors, for example, representatives from community groups, First Nations people, culturally and linguistically diverse communities and local neighbourhoods; and (3) mediators who act as impartial facilitators who do not have a vested interest in the city-making process.

2. **Design** – The second stage is to examine and understand the local context, including the identification of the involved actor's needs, wants and issues. This allows the coalition to explore the design objectives and develop a common purpose.

3. **Development** – The third stage empowers the coalition to generate ideas, prototype city-making concepts, initiatives and policies and test these with each other. This also provides an opportunity to refine the design requirements and reiterate based on the data collected during the process.

4. **Deployment** – The fourth stage incorporates the deployment of the design intervention and facilitates decision-making within the coalition around the city-making topic. This is a continuous process that involves the coalition in the post-deployment phase as new requirements, needs and issues emerge.

Collaborative City-making and Media Architecture as Future Partners

Creating connections, incorporating cultural and local perspectives and understanding people's desires are fundamental in fostering equitable relationships in collaborative city-making. The Middle-out Design Framework has the potential to be applied across various contexts and scales of collaborative city-making and media architecture. This may include any type of engagement and deployment involving intermediation between different groups of people in the decision-making process.

Media architecture can play a number of significant roles in the future of collaborative city-making. These include and are not limited to:

> **Facilitator:** enabling a diverse range of actors to engage with the media architecture interventions as a mechanism to be involved in collaborative city-making.

> **Voice:** expressing cultural and/or societal statements, creative works, knowledge, questions and aspirations.

> **Representation:** implementing policy, infrastructure, interactions and experiences derived by collaborative city-making.

When designing media architecture projects or interventions, oftentimes the role they will take in a collaborative city-making process does not become apparent until the involved actors come together as a coalition and move through the stages of the Middle-out Design Framework. By acknowledging the role the project takes on—whether as facilitator, voice or representation—the attributes, factors and characteristics of the project can be dialled up or dialled down depending on what the coalition needs to achieve their goals and their design aspirations.

Facilitating Collaborative City-making with Media Architecture

Media architecture has an opportunity to play a key role in collaborative city-making by facilitating engagement with top-down and bottom-up actors, providing a voice for cultural and societal expression, and representing interactions, experiences and infrastructure. Two creative examples are discussed here that addressed social isolation and included a diverse mix of people applying collaborative city-making through media architecture interventions.

The Chatty Bench Project

The Chatty Bench Project[3] is an example of a media architecture design intervention that exemplifies how representatives from the top-down and the bottom-up collaborated in the city-making process. Researchers from the Queensland University of Technology worked as facilitators to bring the involved actors together with the aim of addressing social isolation and loneliness of people in the local community. Top-down collaboration came from an owners' corporation committee comprising property owners and bottom-up collaboration from people from the local community, the neighbourhood centre and the village church. This project employed art, performance and locative media to enable community members, predominantly from marginalised communities, to create and engage in critical digital storytelling as part of a hybrid (physical and digital) and radical placemaking process advocating for social justice. Based on a DIY media architecture approach, the Chatty Bench Project engaged with creators via Google classroom, Twine and Hubs by Mozilla to introduce them to digital storytelling practices, interactive technologies and tools, in order to host virtual and in-person exhibitions. Overall, the project not only revealed the critical stories of the creators regarding their experiences facing social isolation but also activated often overlooked public spaces. This was achieved through the

3 - Gonsalves, K., Foth, M., & Caldwell, G. A. (2021, June). Chatty Bench Project: Radical Media Architecture during COVID-19 Pandemic. In M. de Waal. *MAB20: Media Architecture Biennale 20*. Amsterdam and Utrecht, The Netherlands (pp. 182–183). Association for Computing Machinery.

creative design, development and deployment of media architecture with people that created new place experiences within their local neighbourhood.

SP_Urban Arte Conecta

The artist collective, SP_Urban Arte Conecta (p. 144) is an example of a media architecture intervention driven by bottom-up representatives of the local community. In 2020, Brazil encountered a health crisis caused by the COVID-19 pandemic, which exacerbated the country's already severe economic and political crises. People locked in their homes resorted to banging pots and pans in protest of circumstances caused by a troubled government. SP_Urban Arte Conecta emerged at a time when cultural centres and urban nightlife had come to a standstill, while the balconies of apartments became front-row seating for guerrilla urban media interventions and urban projections as new forms of protest. Via an online network, a collective emerged consisting of artists and residents with the São Paulo City Hall to disseminate public health messages in support of the public health system while defending civic rights. This media architecture example demonstrates how the SP_Urban Arte Conecta was more than a festival or collective of media artists; it acted as a middle-out facilitator and, in collaboration with the local government, the City Hall and the local residents, was able to foster a sense of community and wellbeing through artistic means. Through their online presence, the SP_Urban Arte Conecta was co-ordinated and inclusive in its approach to sharing the voice of the people across the landscapes of four Brazilian cities, across the buildings and across the community.

Enhancing Future Collaborative City-making Partnerships

The Chatty Bench Project mentioned earlier took on the role of facilitator. The project worked to bring the decision-makers closer to and more aware of the challenges that the local community were facing in terms of social isolation. Having the role of voice, the SP_Urban Arte Conecta used the words from artists and residents as the artwork and urban projections displayed across the city. The large scale and reach of the projections made the voices pronounced and undeniable. The roles mentioned here are only the beginning of a long list of the many roles which media architecture plays and will continue to take on as cities and involved actors evolve and new partnerships emerge.

Cities are comprised of a mix of many nationalities, ethnicities and cultures, where a variety of different types of people blend together. People all have different requirements, perspectives and needs for how the city they live in should be. Addressing their diverse interests and including their voices in the response to ever-increasing economic, political, social and environmental challenges in city-making is complex. The approach requires strategies such as the Middle-out Design Framework and creative, technologically nuanced interventions provided by media architecture to increase participation and collaboration with people.

Urban Commons

The (urban) commons is a broadly used term referring to a 'third way'—beyond market and state—for the management and stewardship of communal resources, varying from energy and housing to food production and the activation of public spaces. Commons can be distinguished from other organisational models or social regimes by the following factors: they are based on use-value and sustainable or regenerative stewardship rather than market-value and extraction; they focus on care, social relations and personal growth rather than economic transactions and growth; and they are governed based on user-sovereignty. Commons are often presented as an alternative direction for future cities that could make them more sustainable and equitable and allow citizens to claim their 'right to the city'. Media architecture applications can play an instrumental role in the formation and management of urban commons.

Traditional Commons and Their History

The current surge in attention for the commons has been influenced by the work of Elinor Ostrom, who was awarded the Nobel Prize in Economic Sciences in 2009. Ostrom showed that beyond the market and the state, there is a 'third way' to use and manage resources—by communities that have developed sets of rules and social practices to ensure fair usage and distribution of a resource while preventing its depletion.[1] While studying mostly traditional communities around the world and their common-pool resources, such as fishing grounds, forests and meadows, she found that these commons were organised around a set of eight principles. These include the need to set clear group boundaries (who is a member of the community); to develop a system for monitoring, rewarding and punishing behaviour that contributes to or harms the common interest; to include all community members in the democratic governance of the commons; and to introduce a mechanism for conflict resolution.

1 - Ostrom, E. (1990). *Governing the Commons: The Evolution of Institutions for Collective Action*. Cambridge University Press.

Historian Peter Linebaugh has shown that commons predate capitalism and the modern state. Already in the *Charter of the Forest*, a supplementary document to England's *Magna Carta* written in 1217, rights to use the forest were given to the common people. From the 15th century onwards, with the emergence of capitalism, common grounds were increasingly enclosed and privatised. During that process, the commons lost much of its potential as an integrated, regenerative arrangement for social and economic organisation. More recently, modern economic theory criticised the commons, arguing that individuals seeking private gains would deplete the collective resource, inducing a 'tragedy of the commons.'

The value of Ostrom's work lies in her showing that commons are not just a public resource, open for unrestricted private use, but depend on intricate social mechanisms and institutionalised practices for distribution, stewardship and governance: a process sometimes also called 'commoning'. Under these conditions, the commons has proven to be a successful model for managing resources in more sustainable and socially inclusive ways.

New Commons

The last two decades have seen a renewed interest in the commons and commoning as an alternative socio-economic model. This is exemplified by a broad and varied set of initiatives, ranging from energy communities consisting of citizens generating their own renewable energy and neighbourhood wi-fi systems to knowledge commons such as Wikipedia, social solidarity schemes including local currencies, and socially and economically inclusive co-housing developments. These initiatives have been called 'the new commons'.[2] What they share is that they seek to organise alternative ways to manage, steward and

2 - Hess, C. (2008). *Mapping the New Commons*. https://dlc.dlib.indiana.edu/dlc/bitstream/handle/10535/304/Mapping_the_NewCommons.pdf

govern shared resources based on prosocial and sustainable principles and a logic of collaboration and cooperation. Hess sees these initiatives as a reaction to 'increasing commodification, privatization, and corporatization, untamed globalization, and unresponsive governments.' Instead, these movements call upon citizens 'to develop new forms of self-governance, collaboration, and collective action.'

Like traditional commons, new commons cannot be understood as separate from the commoners (the community managing the resource) and the process of commoning. The social interactions, management tasks and governance processes carried out by the commoners are aimed at the regenerative use of the resource as well as the building and maintenance of the community around it.

Urban Commons

A number of authors have more specifically started to speak of 'the urban commons', defined by Dellenbaugh-Losse et al.[3] as 'resources in the city which are managed by the users in a non-profit-oriented and prosocial way'. What sets urban commons apart from traditional commons is that cities are complex forms of social organisation, with a broad variety of people, with broadly varying interests, and a volatile population of residents, commuters, visitors, tourists, refugees, etc. This makes it difficult to set boundaries and establish informal arrangements for inclusive practices of commoning. Hence, Dellenbaugh-Losse et al. have found that commons projects in urban environments often need 'custodians', in the form of (semi) professionals who take a leading role in assembling a community around a resource. Here, transparency and accountability are of great importance to ensure the sovereignty of the commoners at large.

3 - Dellenbaugh-Losse, M., Zimmermann, N.-E., & de Vries, N. (2020). *The Urban Commons Cookbook: Strategies and Insights for Creating and Maintaining Urban Commons*. http://urbancommonscookbook.com

Another point is that cities themselves are complex assemblages of various governance regimes, public, collective and private. Cities are formally and informally governed by locally set laws as well as customs and long-standing cultural practices. Civic initiatives, government programmes, commercial activities, non-governmental organisations (NGOs) and individual citizens all play a role in the functioning of the city. Urban commons need to relate themselves to all of these actors and activities to carve out their own space and practices of operation. This is sometimes also called a 'hacking mentality': appropriating and tinkering with existing practices and technological and legal infrastructures to turn them to the advantage of a commons.

Three Ways to Understand the Urban Commons

Urban commons are understood as 'common property regimes'.[4] These concern exclusive, usually depletable, resources that are clearly bounded, with defined sets of formal rights or informal practices that regulate access, usage and privileges for its members. They are sometimes also called resource communities. Examples of these resource communities include:

4 - Foster, S. R., & Iaione, C. (2019). Ostrom in the City: Design Principles and Practices for the Urban Commons. In B. Hudson, J. Rosenbloom & D. Cole (Eds.), *Routledge Handbook of the Study of the Commons* (pp. 235–255). Routledge.

> **Mobility communities** share mobility resources: e-cars, cargo bikes, trailers, charging infrastructures, etc.

> **Building and housing communities** develop houses for their own needs with customised flats and common spaces for leisure activities, sports, cultural activities, home office, etc.

> **Energy communities** jointly construct energy generation and distribute the energy (electricity or heat) among the members of the community.

Various authors have specified a set of rights that are either formally or informally encoded in these commons. These include: access (who can enter the commons and enjoy its benefits); extraction (who has what rights or privileges to obtain subtractive elements of the resource); management (who has the right to participate in the setting of the rules and the governance process); exclusion (who determines which outsiders can join or reap benefits from the commons); and alienation (the right to sell some of these rights to others).

In the setting up of these resource communities, various tensions may emerge between the commons-based community and its relation to the city at large. To what extent does a resource community contribute to public values for the city at large, and is it an enabler for the building of social relations and personal growth beyond the community itself? Are there clear and just rules for becoming a member? If not, these common property resources run the risk of becoming collective private resources or even gated communities.

A second category of urban commons takes the shape of collaborative actions in which citizens claim their 'right to the city' around non-exclusive resources, such as public space or neglected private properties. Examples are initiatives in which citizens start running activities in public spaces, take part in the upkeep of public parks or set up a collective urban gardening or farming project on a vacant lot. Compared to common property arrangements, access to these resources (e.g. public space) is usually non-exclusive. 'Membership' or participation is a much more open-ended process, and these practices of commoning are even more intertwined with existing regimes governing resources.

In a third approach, the term (urban) commons is invoked as a philosophical concept in the context of political theory and the field of law. In this way it could be used as a foundation for thinking about societies and justice and operationalised in the legal systems that assign rights and duties. For instance, when we start thinking of the city as a commons it opens pathways for legal interpretation or reform that shifts a legal regime favouring the safeguarding of individual property rights to one that prioritises public values and societal wellbeing at large.

Media Architecture and the Commons

Media architecture can play a role in the commoning process in at least three ways. First, media architecture can be designed to visualise urban resources in public spaces that potentially could be organised as a commons and associate them with prospective publics. Media architecture is often designed to visualise (or make them experienceable otherwise) collective rhythms or issues, allowing for identification and the formation of urban publics. Examples include Yellow Dust, exhibited in Seoul, South Korea, which made air pollution visible and tactile in public spaces. In Montreal, the project Megaphone used projection mapping to visualise the concerns of passers-by on a large facade. In Kenya the Civic Design Data Lab used GPS trackers to map the routes of local minibuses, *matatus*, used as public transport, publishing for the first time a public transport map for them and also framing them as a system rather than a loose collection of individual routes.

Second, in a more interactive modality, media architecture can also be designed to incite debates about the (governance of the) commons. For instance, Citizen Dialog Kit (p. 140) consists of a system of distributed screens throughout a neighbourhood that can be used to organise polls. In Queensland, Australia the installation InstaBooth was introduced in several public spaces to engage citizens in a public dialogue by inviting them into a private booth. It is expected that digital platforms such as Decidim will play an important enabling role in the establishment of commons, as they are powerful digital infrastructures that could be used for consultation and social formation, providing information about options to join commoning activities.

Third, digital platforms can play a role in the actual coordination of commoning processes. Sensors could automatically monitor resource production and usage, and algorithms could match supply and demand. It is thought that blockchain technology will play a particularly important role.[5] As blockchain technologies are built around decentralised immutable databases, they are seen as particularly fit to administer resource production usage and contributions. So-called smart contracts can distribute usage rights amongst participants. It is argued that making contributions and usage transparent on such a system could help counter 'free riding' and the tragedy of the commons. However, as Cila et al.[6] have shown, the design of digital platforms for resource communities is a complex affair. Though they are often seen as mere management systems, they function as systems that govern the commons; particular values and preferences are encoded in algorithms and decisions on what to measure and what to leave off-chain influence the commoning process. In the projects mentioned above, media architecture becomes an active part of a commons. Its interfaces and software encode particular values related to the commons, giving it an active mediating role in the commoning process itself.

5 - Rozas, D., Tenorio-Fornés, A., Díaz-Molina, S., & Hassan, S. (2021). When Ostrom Meets Blockchain: Exploring the Potentials of Blockchain for Commons Governance. *Sage Open, 11*(1).

6 - Cila, N., Ferri, G., de Waal, M., Gloerich, I., & Karpinski, T. (2020, April). The Blockchain and the Commons: Dilemmas in the Design of Local Platforms. In *CHI '20: Proceedings of the 2020 CHI Conference on Human Factors in Computing Systems*, Honolulu, United States (1–14). Association for Computing Machinery.

Autonomous Agents

Ridley Scott's 1982 science fiction classic *Blade Runner* has been cited as an inspiration for media architecture on numerous occasions, as previously discussed. For many, this will immediately call to mind a dystopian cityscape of futuristic buildings that function as large-scale advertising screens. Today, we can witness media facades—an instantiation of the concept of buildings as screens—around the globe, and they have certainly been a catalyst for the emergence of media architecture as a field. However, media facades are not the only advanced urban technology shaping the distinctive mise en scène of *Blade Runner* and, at the same time, providing visionary potential for media architecture. What about, for example, the flying cars and replicants depicting a speculative urban robotic future?

Currently, we are still a long way off from calling flying cars our preferred mode of transport (although plans exist to ferry people around South East Queensland, Australia with autonomous flying taxis during the 2032 Olympics). Also, our streets are not occupied (yet) by humanoid robots whose external appearance is indistinguishable from non-engineered humans. However, the automation and robotisation of cities has gained considerable pace over the past few years, with cities such as San Francisco, Tokyo and Dubai acting as testbed environments for experimentation with autonomous agents.[1] Example applications range from autonomous vehicles that transport humans, to smaller mobile robots for automating public services and the delivery of goods.

Admittedly, at first glance, those applications seem to have little in common with the early protagonists of media architecture, such as urban screens and media facades. However, the field has evolved over the years, with designers and researchers turning to new emerging technologies and now creating artefacts of various shapes and scales. Media architecture can now be considered as a framework to guide the design and development of physical spaces and interfaces, thereby not only considering technological but also aesthetic, social and ethical concerns. Similar to the way in which media architecture has sought to respond to the proliferation of digital media in cities, it is now necessary to turn to new matters, such as artificial intelligence (AI) and urban robotics.[2] Discussing the notion of autonomous agents in relation to media architecture, this chapter sheds light on the opportunities to create new media architectural interfaces as well as how media architecture as a framework can guide the responsible integration of autonomous agents into cities.

Autonomous Agents as Cyber-physical City Applications

Long before the establishment of media architecture as a research field, architects approached topics such as automation, mobility and AI through visionary proposals for cybernetic interfaces and robotised systems. These radical visions of 1960s and 70s architectural groups have cast their long shadows and still provide thought and inspiration. The avant-garde architectural group Archigram, for instance, created the vision of the 'Walking City'. Their iconic collages depict giant self-contained pods roaming around the natural environment in order to exchange resources and services for their inhabitants. Other examples are those from the Italian design collective Superstudio, who envisioned a city with a shared infrastructure that removes the pressing need for owning personal objects. This is, in light of limited global resources, a desirable goal which is now slowly shifting towards extended realities; new shared mobility concepts have emerged which are only

1 - While, A. H., Marvin, S., & Kovacic, M. (2020). Urban robotic experimentation: San Francisco, Tokyo and Dubai. *Urban Studies, 58*(4), 769–786.

2 - Wiethoff, A., Hoggenmueller, M., Rossmy, B., Hirsch, L., Hespanhol, L., & Tomitsch, M. (2021). A Media Architecture Approach for Designing the Next Generation of Urban Interfaces. *IxD&A, 48*, 9–32.

the forerunners of a shared urban infrastructure relying on autonomous agents that is yet to come.

Today's urban robotic landscape might not appear radical in its manifestation when compared to the above-mentioned visions. Rather than monolithic pods that function as cities, we see the design and implementation of manoeuvrable autonomous agents of smaller scale, such as delivery robots, that will be scattered across the city. Earlier, the concept of the city as software was introduced, thereby considering two perspectives: the city as an operating system and media architectural interventions as city apps. These perspectives are useful to understand the current (and likely future) approach towards autonomous agents in cities, as well as their relation to media architecture.

The city as the operating system provides the necessary urban infrastructure for autonomous agents to operate. This can be physical infrastructure, such as pavements for a mobile robot to commute, or digital infrastructure, such as communication networks for a delivery robot to connect to its customer. Importantly, while terms such as 'robot cities' misleadingly suggest that robots will *make up* what is referred to as a 'city', they are only (temporarily) using our city infrastructure and extending it through services that they offer. On that note, the large-scale rollout of autonomous agents will certainly bring infrastructural changes. However, the city as our operating system needs to remain compatible beyond robots, considering human and environmental needs. For example, the rollout of mobile robots should not disrupt existing urban activities, such as the way humans move. Instead, autonomous agents should use these activities as input to develop pedestrian-friendly behaviour. Greg Lynn, architect and CEO of the robotics company Piaggio Fast Forward, calls this a 'robot with etiquette'.[3]

In the context of the city, robotic and automation technologies have so far largely operated in the background. The autonomous agents described here are defined by their physical manifestation, their direct

3 - Lynn, G. (2020, January 11). *Robot Etiquette: Designing Autonomous Machines for Pedestrian Spaces.* Medium. https://medium.com/@formgreglynn/robot-etiquette-6509abc92e32

↑ A movable city lighting concept developed by Felix Dietz, Oliver Hein and Lars Wüstemann.

interplay with the physical urban environment and their purpose to serve and interact with the end user, the citizen. The notion of city apps describes the enhancement of urban experiences through the integration of digital technology into the built environment and existing urban artefacts. Adding intelligence and autonomy to this, autonomous agents can be thought of as cyber-physical city apps. For example, a park bench could be extended through conversational AI capabilities and anthropomorphic features, thus functioning as a companion in addition to serving the purpose of seating. A smart, interactive rubbish bin could be further extended to autonomously change its position, allowing the bin to temporarily relocate to areas where increased littering is expected to happen (e.g. during a street festival) and even dispose of garbage independently at a central collection point. In this sense, robotics and AI can extend the meaning and functionality of traditional urban artefacts and digital city apps, thus expanding the design space of media architectural interventions. This paradigm shift allows us to consider media architecture as not being bound to geographical locations and remaining there immutable until its deconstruction. Instead, it forces us to think of cities as complex organic systems that have the ability to alter certain extremities and shapes according to changed behaviour patterns. Designers and architects, therefore, have to consider this design space more holistically and utilise novel prototyping approaches in order to create life-centric solutions for the people, as exemplified through inspirational cases in the following section.

Media Architecture Approaches Towards Autonomous Agents

There are now an increasing number of examples from media architecture research and education that have turned to autonomous agents as a vehicle for prototyping emerging media architectural interfaces. They make use of actuators or self-moving platforms, such as mobile ground robots and drones.[4] Often, these projects still incorporate some type of lighting technology and address media architecture core themes, such as playfulness, engagement and participation.

4 - Hoggenmueller, M., Hespanhol, L., & Tomitsch, M. (2020, April). Stop and Smell the Chalk Flowers: a Robotic Probe for Investigating Urban Interaction with Physicalised Displays. In CHI '20 *Proceedings of the 2020 CHI Conference on Human Factors in Computing Systems*. Honolulu, United States of America (pp. 1–14). Association for Computing Machinery.

In the context of a design studio course at the University of Munich, teams of interdisciplinary students from architecture and human-computer interaction (HCI) prototyped novel design solutions for movable city lighting. The exploratory projects were carried out over one semester in collaboration with the lighting design company Ingo Maurer. One media architectural prototype, JellyLight, explored the idea of flying lamps inspired by fireflies. The organic shaped objects incorporate flexible, moveable elements that can adapt and change their pattern, aiming to act as mediators between people and the urban environment. Based on presence, proximity and other possible influencing factors, such as weather, temperature and lighting conditions, the autonomous object represents a fusion of digital media and moveable city lighting design. The prototypes also raised the question of whether modular lighting objects should be used for personal or shared purposes by residents. The interplay of artistic design elements with specific usage scenarios played a decisive role in the contextual design, as the lighting system has been developed for a city park that is surrounded by a student residential complex and many shops and restaurants. These early explorations and prototypes can serve as manifestations of design ideas for next generation media architectural interventions that act as autonomous agents in a shared city economy.

Another example is the urban robot Woodie (p. 196). Woodie is a slow-moving urban robot that draws with conventional chalk sticks on the ground and is equipped with low-resolution LEDs in its outer shell to attract and communicate with passers-by. The fully functional prototype was deployed for three weeks during the annual lighting festival Vivid Sydney, drawing simple sketches, such as flowers and love hearts, on a laneway. Chalk sticks were handed out to surrounding people so they could extend and add to the robot's drawings. Not only the collaborative activity itself but also Woodie's presence and appearance—which resulted in people perceiving it as a living being—attracted considerable attention and interest from the public. The prototype is a good example of how autonomous agents as cyber-physical city apps can temporarily turn ordinary laneways into places of playful participation and engagement, while not disrupting other urban activities or making permanent changes to the surrounding environment.

Opportunities Emerging from Autonomous Agents

Media architecture refers to built structures and physical spaces that incorporate media (in any form) to facilitate communication with the public. It is an emerging field that continues to evolve as technology advances. Designing autonomous agents for and in the city provides exciting new opportunities for media architecture researchers and practitioners.

Autonomous agents as cyber-physical city apps represent a form of embodied AI. In this sense, their physical manifestation—having a direct interplay with the immediate urban environment unlike machine learning algorithms running on remote server farms—corresponds nicely with

↑ Woodie exhibited at Vivid Sydney 2019. (Media credit: Marius Hoggenmüller.)

media architects' long-term vision of a fusion of digital technologies and physical urban spaces.

Here, autonomous agents are not only defined by their embodied representation but also by their ability to perform physical movements. As motion induces the perception of animacy, in particular if inspired by the motion characteristics of living organisms, there is an opportunity for media architecture to create more affective interactions and experiences. Instead of interacting with digital media content, autonomous agents can induce in people the feeling of interacting with a non-human mediator or agent. In the case of Woodie, people even reportedly referred to the robot as though it were a living being.

Due to their flexibility and ad hoc deployment, autonomous agents such as JellyLight and Woodie can enhance the experience of underutilised public spaces or create new ones. Conceptually speaking, they can use the city as an operating system in an even more versatile manner. They represent a new strategy for digital placemaking that does not come with the burdens and costs associated with the permanent deployment of present digital placemaking platforms, such as public displays or media facades. This might also benefit segregated urban neighbourhoods, which in particular suffer from lower collective investments and public goods expenditures.

Considering the aforementioned shifts and new paradigms, there is a pressing need to define processes and use a design language that is both aesthetic and understandable. How should autonomous agents look and be seamlessly integrated with the city? There is a risk in leaving this question entirely to big-tech corporations, which have the resources to develop and deploy the necessary technology on a large scale. On the other hand, an integrative design approach based on media architectural principles has the ability to align stakeholder interests while designing with and for the people. Due to the emergence of more affective media architecture applications and systems, there is an even stronger urgency for a common vocabulary and pattern language to make systems internationally comprehensible.

While the presented examples here have strong similarities with traditional media architecture interventions in their aesthetics and meaning, media architecture approaches and principles could be applied in a wider range of cyber-physical city apps, including in more mundane application contexts, such as mobility and food supply. With its multidisciplinary approach, media architecture offers knowledge in regards to responsible urban innovation and keeping all stakeholders in the loop, which includes, in the context of the city, users and non-users. 'Keeping the human in the loop' is a broad term commonly used in AI research communities; however, it also applies to cyber-physical city apps: when deploying more autonomous-decision-making processes in the urban context, people still need to be able to understand and intervene if necessary.

More-than-human Futures

Interaction design scholars have engaged with environmental issues and sustainability concerns for more than two decades. Early attempts were mainly borrowed from psychology and seek to 'persuade' users and influence their behaviour towards more ethical and environmentally friendly consumption choices, such as conserving energy, avoiding single-use plastic products and increasing overall resource efficiencies. However, the underlying focus on usability and thus 'the user' mostly remained unchanged, which has been critiqued, drawing attention to the political and institutional arena and calling for greater systemic change and impact.

Yet, the 'user' paradigm—so fundamental in both design and media architecture—has not only been criticised for its singularity but also for its humanness, that is, its human exceptionalism. But how did this come about? In the 1950s, 'human factors' as a field of research was inspired by the poor usability derived from traditional technocentric approaches to technology engineering and development, as part of a concern for improving aeroplane safety. This went hand in hand with the advent of human-centred design when Professor John E. Arnold founded the design program at Stanford University in 1958, teaching engineering students to use human-centred design approaches. As a response to the original limitations of technology-led engineering, human-centred design offered a lot of merit and value. However, human-centred design—especially when embedded in a commercial context—tends to focus on products and services that favour human comfort and convenience at the expense of fauna, flora and the planet, with some going so far as to argue that designers have destroyed the world.

In response—and in parallel to the trend to use design methods not just for usability but for scale and impact—another related development has emerged that is best characterised as a posthumanist approach: the more-than-human turn in design,[1] architecture, urban planning and built environment,[2] and media architecture.[3] The more-than-human perspective recognises the human exceptionalism implicit in most conventional design approaches and proposes to level the field by decentring the human and proposing new methods to engage and 'design with' the more-than-human world. Beyond a concern for the environment or commitment to sustainability and beyond the human-centred city, more-than-human media architecture is thus an approach to creating and designing with a post-anthropocentric lens.

Since the initial paper from the Media Architecture Biennale (MAB) 2018, where the more-than-human concept and its implications for media architecture was first presented[3], there have been some significant responses and initiatives that demonstrate the impact of this approach on the community of practice surrounding the Biennale. The MAB of 2020/21 was scheduled for June 2020; however, due to the global COVID-19 pandemic, MAB was postponed until 2021, creating even more time for practitioners, designers and researchers to grapple with the state of the world and the climate crisis. The Media Architecture Awards that are part of every MAB event welcomed and acknowledged more-than-human media architecture as its own category for the first time, and nine submissions were received from the following countries: The Netherlands,

1 - Forlano, L. (2017). Posthumanism and Design. *She Ji: The Journal of Design, Economics, and Innovation, 3*(1), 16–29.

2 - Fieuw, W., Foth, M., & Caldwell, G. A. (2022). Towards a More-than-Human Approach to Smart and Sustainable Urban Development: Designing for Multispecies Justice. *Sustainability, 14*(2), 948.

3 - Foth, M., & Caldwell, G. (2018). More-than-Human media architecture. In C. Zhigang (Ed.), *MAB 18: Proceedings of the 4th Media Architecture Biennale Conference*. Beijing, China (pp. 66–75). Association for Computing Machinery.

China, France, Finland, Austria and Germany. The nominees from the more-than-human award category feature in the 'Practice' part of this book. The more-than-human theme also featured as a key area of research in the call for papers and the workshops and events that led up to the Biennale. More-than-human media architecture is more than a category or an approach to research; it is a fundamental way for designers and architects to consider how and why the projects they create respond to the needs of not just humans but non-human beings too.

The original more-than-human media architecture paper at MAB' 18 largely focused on reducing harm as a first step. For example, many media facades and media architecture installations by their very nature comprise ubiquitous computing and IoT devices and LEDs or public screens and displays. In addition to their energy consumption and the associated carbon footprint, these electronic components cause harm during manufacture, use and disposal, including the unregulated mining of rare earth metals in some parts of the world, light pollution affecting insects, birds and nocturnal animals, and risk of entanglements with wires and e-waste[3]. While reducing harm is commendable, it does not go far enough, and commentators have started to call for a net-positive or nature-positive approach to designing the built environment.[4] Additionally, the more-than-human pivot in design prompts the appropriation of existing approaches as well as the development of new methods, e.g. non-human personas.

4 - Birkeland, J. (2022). Nature Positive: Interrogating Sustainable Design Frameworks for Their Potential to Deliver Eco-Positive Outcomes. *Urban Science, 6*(2), 35.

Examples of More-than-human Design Approaches

Three exemplary projects are presented that reveal different ways of thinking, questioning, highlighting or responding to the compelling proposition that the more-than-human brings to media architecture.

The first one is called Active Living Infrastructure: Controlled Environment (ALICE),[5] led by Professor Rachel Armstrong as part of a research consortium with Newcastle University, the University of the West of England and Translating Nature. They have created a prototype of living bricks that can generate energy by connecting humans with microbes. The living bricks can form walls or structures while also creating a bio-digital interface and artistic installation. The bricks contain microbes that transform liquid waste, such as urine, into the electricity it needs to run itself and power LEDs and the soundscape it generates. The bricks include biosensors which record data of the microbial electrons. ALICE fuses biological and digital technologies to monitor if the microbes need feeding and how healthy they are. Similar to a Tamagotchi, or digital pet, the data gathered by the sensors and performance of the microbes is conveyed to users via interactive displays, which communicate if they require feeding or temperature regulation to improve their ability to generate bioelectricity. The main goal of the project is to create interactive displays to visualise what the microbes are doing based on the data that is captured, creating a trans-species communication platform that allows people to deepen their understanding and appreciation for Microbial Fuel Cells. This project combines biology with technology to create innovative and bio-based construction materials, which take a step towards minimising the need for fossil fuels by providing energy for buildings. ALICE is an example of how architects, designers and researchers can work to establish co-dependent relationships with nature for the benefit of more-than-humans. The project is experienced either via the online interface or as a physical installation.

The second example is the Schumacher Quartier in Berlin, Germany. The decommissioned Tegel Airport in Berlin is being transformed by the State of Berlin and the Tegel Projekt GmbH with the aim to develop a carbon neutral, environmentally friendly residential community, the Schumacher Quartier, and a research precinct, Berlin TXL—The Urban Tech Republic. At Berlin TXL urban technologies will be researched and developed based on smart

5 - ALICE. (n.d.). *alice: active living infrastructure: controlled environment.* University of the West of England, Translating Nature and University of Newcastle. Retrieved January 3, 2023, from https://www.alice-interface.eu

↑ Fairy light installation deployed on mangrove trees at the entrance of the Goodwill Bridge, Brisbane, Australia. (Media credit: Marcus Foth.)

city concepts and a real-world laboratory addressing six core themes: net zero energy systems, environmentally friendly transportation, clean water, recycling, new materials for sustainable construction and networked control systems. Although the Tegel Projekt is not necessarily a media architecture exemplar, it will have interactive technologies embedded in the development for a range of purposes, including for monitoring of traffic systems and building performance (e.g. energy performance), and for entertainment via digital screens. What is of interest here is their use of Animal-Aided Design (AAD), which aims to integrate the habitat needs of animal species into the design workflow to use as planning aids for landscape architects, architects and planners. AAD is a key approach for how the Tegel Projekt will address biodiversity as a fundamental planning principle. With many parallels to a more-than-human approach, Animal-Aided Design intends to create habitats and refuge for diverse animal species within the buildings and landscapes that are created as part of built environments.

The third example is the Living Building Challenge (LBC). As the digital and electronic components of media architecture projects and installations are embedded in the physical layers of the built environment, they are subject to performance assessment tools. Well-established green building rating tools, such as Leadership in Energy and Environmental Design (LEED), Building Research Establishment Environmental Assessment Method (BREEAM), WELL Building Standard® and Green Star focus too much on energy alone at the expense of other prospective criteria and factors. By asking 'What if every single act of design and construction made the world a better place?', LBC[6] stands out as a more progressive framework that is closer to the aforementioned aspiration for a net-positive or climate-positive approach to the design of the built environment. Rather than a sole focus on energy, the LBC is more encompassing by including six additional requirements: place, materials, equity, water, beauty, and health and happiness.

6 - International Living Future Institute (n.d.) *Living Building Challenge*. Retrieved January 3, 2023, from https://living-future.org/lbc

42 / CONCEPTS / MORE-THAN-HUMAN FUTURES

While the LBC still largely focuses on traditional, that is, physical/tangible architecture, there is a timely opportunity to translate the aspirations and requirements of the LBC to guide media architecture practitioners as well.

From Human-centred to Life-centred Design

With increasing pressures from climate change, biodiversity loss and an accelerating pace towards a planetary ecocide, large parts of the media architecture community struggle to identify meaningful responses. How can media architecture research and practice contribute ethically and constructively to dealing with the climate emergency? These concerns are shared by the architecture, design and human-computer interaction communities more broadly. Avoiding the limits of technological solutionism, the more-than-human design approach entails an ontological and epistemological shift away from human-centred and towards life-centred design. While this paradigm has a long tradition in the environmental humanities and reflects Indigenous and First Nations thinking, aspects of it are starting to be translated into mainstream practices of industry and government. For example, for the first time the International Olympic Committee requires the Brisbane 2032 Olympic Games to not only be climate-neutral but actually climate-positive. This requirement has real implications and repercussions for any designer, service provider and stakeholder wanting to participate and contribute to this large-scale event. It also illustrates how some of these theoretical ideas are slowly finding their way into everyday design practices.

METHODS

pose, when and where it is best applied and how it can be used for media architecture. The section is organised into four categories—Research, Design, Prototype and Deployment— making it easy for readers to find the method that best suits their needs.

The methods are based on the experience of the authors and contributors, who have used and studied these methods through design projects, research explorations and teaching. They offer a unique perspective on how each method can contribute to the advancement of media architecture and promote new ways of thinking about the intersection of digital technology and physical space.

The section provides a valuable resource for those looking to expand their knowledge of media architecture methods. It caters for students, researchers, practitioners and professionals, providing them with a valuable and accessible reference for their work. The practical steps for using each method are provided via the book's companion website (mac2.mediaarchitecture.org), making it easy to put the concepts into practice.

Urban Probes
Exploring the complexity of decisions and experiences in and with the city

1 - Eric Paulos, E. & Tom Jenkins, T. (2005). Urban probes: Encountering our emerging urban atmospheres. In *CHI '05: Proceedings of the SIGCHI Conference on Human Factors in Computing Systems* (CHI '05). Portland, United States (pp. 341–350). Association for Computing Machinery.

The notion of urban probes describes a design and research method that uses unconventional or provocative design artefacts to prompt people to engage with and reflect on experiences within our everyday urban environment. Paulos and Jenkins[1] first described Urban Probes as provocative interventions that explore new technologies for urban space, similar to the method of 'Technology Probes'. Beyond exploring new technologies in urban spaces, urban probes also include qualities drawn from 'Cultural Probes', which are used for prompt reflection and in-situ understanding of peoples' lives.

Urban probes are best for exploring research topics in which locations, physical surroundings and everyday experiences play a significant role in the topics of interest. Urban probes allow designers and researchers to explore new ideas and investigate experiences and activities that are a part of our environment that we might not always notice or recognise.

The implementation of urban probes may be in the form of paper printouts or may use lightweight electronic components, such as microcontrollers, LED screens, buttons, sensors or microphones. Urban probes use these components to provide prompts and record stories digitally or to explore and evaluate new design ideas.

Urban probes can be designed in various shapes or forms. However, the scale of an urban probe artefact does play a significant role in the type of provocation that is facilitated and the type of response that is elicited. For instance, a smaller-scale urban probe that engages with one or two people at the same time could facilitate intimate conversations, while media architecture interventions on a building scale may have a wider reach.

↑ Site-specific design ideation

Urban probes should be designed to allow the uncertainty of play and exploration. People may respond to urban probes through their own interpretations. Yet, the unexpected responses or interactions also tell us rich stories about how people's lived experiences influence their perceptions of a place or what is associated with the place for them. Urban probes can be designed to collect data or record information as a part of the interactive experience. The designer and researcher may also conduct observations and interviews to develop a deeper understanding of people's interactions with the urban probe. However, it is important to note the outcome of the urban probe should be viewed through the lens of empathy and not judgement. The outcomes of urban probe studies should be understood but not as binary definitions.

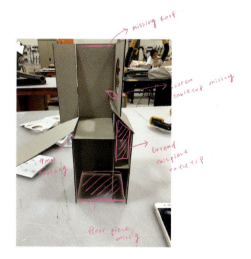

↑↑ Example of urban probe deployment
↑ Lo-fi prototyping

Method Steps ↗
https://mac2.mediaarchitecture.org/methods/probes

Middle-out Workshops
Creating a coalition of ideas to facilitate collaborative decision-making

1 - Caldwell, G. A., Fredericks, J., Hespanhol, L., Chamorro-Koc, M., Barajas, M. J. S. V., & André, M. J. C. (2021). Putting the people back into the "smart": Developing a middle-out framework for engaging citizens. In A. Aurigi & N. Odendaal (Eds.) *Shaping Smart for Better Cities* (1st ed., pp. 239–266). Academic Press.

2 - Fredericks, J., Caldwell, G. A., & Tomitsch, M. (2016, November). Middle-out design: collaborative community engagement in urban HCI. In *OzCHI '16: Proceedings of the 28th Australian Conference on Computer-Human Interaction.* Launceston, Tasmania (pp. 200–204). Association for Computing Machinery.

Middle-out workshops draw on a diverse range of actors to collaboratively work together in the city-making process, which can be used for designing, developing and deploying media architecture interventions. This approach incorporates the objectives, expertise and knowledge of top-down and bottom-up actors to meet in the middle with the purpose to move outward and forward.[1] The mutual advantage of meeting in the middle is common to all partnerships and collaborations. Making compromises to consider the interests, wants and aspirations of different human and non-human actors can create a coalition of ideas to facilitate decision-making for collective action.

Middle-out workshops build on existing co-design and participatory design workshop models by including involved actors in every stage of the process.[2] This includes the planning and design of workshop locations and activities, data collection methods and the analysis of the results. Typically, co-design and participatory design workshops are facilitated in controlled environments, such as design studios and laboratories, whereas middle-out workshops can also be run in urban environments and locations that connect participants directly to the city-making activity.

There are three distinct roles that form part of a middle-out workshop: (1) top-down actors, for example, people working in government agencies that create policy and regulatory requirements or people from industry that drive innovation and development in city infrastructure and technology platforms; (2) bottom-up actors, for example, representatives from community groups, First Nations people, culturally and linguistically diverse communities and local neighbourhoods;

and (3) mediator(s) who acts as a facilitator. The mediator's role is important for communicating with all actors and integrating their objectives into various workshop stages. This suggests that a successful middle-out workshop relies on an independent entity that does not have a direct interest in the workshop outcomes.

Middle-out workshops can be incorporated at any stage of the media architecture development process. In the research phase, they can be used to identify specific needs, circumstances and situations of urban dwellers. For media architecture projects, this includes developing a deep understanding of peoples' connection to place, infrastructure and technology. During the design and prototype phases, middle-out workshops can generate ideas and rapidly iterate concepts, for example, designing and testing a smart city bench or interactive media installation. During the deployment phase, middle-out workshops can continue to include involved actors in post-deployment data analysis and the decision-making process.

↑ Workshop mediator facilitating activities with the coalition in a community garden. (Media credit: Joel Fredericks.)

↑ Coalition representatives prototyping a media architecture installation. (Media credit: Joel Fredericks.)

Method Steps ↗
https://mac2.mediaarchitecture.org/methods/middle-out

Actor Mapping

Identifying who is involved in or affected by a media architecture intervention

↑ Lack of engagement with local communities led to a backlash associated with new advertising screens in Sydney, Australia. (Media credit: Joel Fredericks.)

Traditionally, when designing digital products like software applications, the focus was on users as those that would interact with the final product. Over time, this scope was expanded to also include others, who may not directly interact with the product but either have an indirect stake or may be indirectly affected. We refer to this wider group of entities as 'actors'. In many cases, we can distinguish between primary and secondary actors. For example, viewed through a human-centred design lens, when designing software for health practitioners, doctors and nurses might be the primary actors. But the experience of the patient is also indirectly affected by the software product, making them a secondary actor. As another example, viewed through a project management lens, the client paying for the design of a new product may represent the primary actor. Other entities that have to be considered in the process, such as marketing, legislative authorities and so on, make up the secondary actors.

We can use the same notion in media architecture during the research phase to identify who is involved in or affected by an intervention. This is useful to contribute to the long-term success of a media architecture intervention. For example, if the local community was not adequately considered, there may be a backlash when the intervention is rolled out. Time spent on mapping out the actors and engaging them in the process will pay off later. It is therefore important to include a time and cost allowance for this in the initial project scoping.

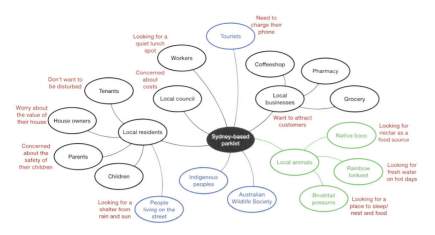

← Example of using actor mapping for a potential parklet design. (Media credit: Martin Tomitsch.)

The method can also be used to bring additional perspectives into the process. For example, this may involve working with First Nations peoples to explore how the media architecture intervention can respond to or highlight cultural traditions associated with the site.[1] The Digital Bricks project (p. 86) illustrates how considering these perspectives can inform the design of a media architecture intervention.

The method further provides a mechanism to consider non-human perspectives by mapping out the non-human entities that may be affected by or that could benefit from the intervention.[2] For example, light-based media architecture interventions may have an adverse effect on nocturnal animals.[3] Identifying non-human actors can also provide a source for design inspiration. For example, visual images of ecosystems were used as content in the Aukio project (p. 110) as a way to connect people walking through a busy airport with nature. As another example, the Monarch Sanctuary building facade designed by Terreform ONE used media architecture to raise awareness about species extinction through amplifying live images of monarch butterflies nesting inside the green facade.

1 - Anderson, S., Wouters, N., & Jefferies, R. (2021, June). Decolonising the Urban Screen: An Argument and Approach for First Peoples-led Content Programs in Massive Media. In *MAB20: Media Architecture Biennale 20*, Amsterdam and Utrecht, The Netherlands (pp. 66–78). Association for Computing Machinery.

2 - Tomitsch, M., Fredericks, J., Vo, D., Frawley, J., & Foth, M. (2021). Non-human Personas: Including Nature in the Participatory Design of Smart Cities. *Interaction Design and Architecture(s)*, *50*, pp. 102–130.

3 - Foth, M., & Caldwell, G. (2018). More-than-Human media architecture. In C. Zhigang (Ed.), *MAB 18: Proceedings of the 4th Media Architecture Biennale Conference* (pp. 66–75). Association for Computing Machinery.

Method Steps ↗
https://mac2.mediaarchitecture.org/methods/actor-mapping

Intermediation Practices

Strategies and tactics for community engagement to achieve mutually beneficial outcomes

Media architecture projects by their very nature tend to be situated in the public realm, commissioned by different clients, require input, support and approvals from institutional entities and funding bodies, and seek to engage a diversity of users and community members. We suggest that dealing competently and successfully with the complexity of this community engagement challenge warrants an explicit and methodical approach: intermediation practice.

Why is this needed? The typical creative process in many media architecture projects already comprises well-established design research and design thinking methods for ideation, conceptualisation, content production, deployment and testing. These methods tend to have in common a focus on creativity, originality, novelty, usability, user experience and, hopefully, eventually client acceptance. While this may be conducive to get creative juices flowing during ideation, these design methods have also been criticised for their limitations of dealing adequately with common institutional constraints. For example, design thinking workshops have been likened to setting up a 'sandbox' environment.[1]

Design visions eventually have to leave this safe space and be implemented by unwieldy government departments or business partners. Lodato and DiSalvo[1] identify some of the potential pitfalls, or 'administration gaps', such as failure to secure ongoing funding for content curation, programming and maintenance post-deployment. Problems can also arise from an ideological mismatch between the values and aspirations imbued during the design phase versus the reality and lived experience of those actors and staff charged with implementing and maintaining the project. A project can be met

1 - Lodato, T., & DiSalvo, C. (2018, August). Institutional constraints: the forms and limits of participatory design in the public realm. In L. Huybrechts, M. Teli, A. Light, Y. Lee, J. Garde, J. Vines, E. Brandt, A. M. Kanstrup, & K. Bødker. *PDC '18: Proceedings of the 15th Participatory Design Conference (PDC 2018)*, Hasselt and Genk, Belgium (pp. 1–12). Association for Computing Machinery.

with pushback if it clashes with more rigid and risk-averse structural hegemonies, vested interests or fiefdoms and their gatekeepers both systemic and human.

Even in the best of situations, without the above blockages, where actors are supportive and keen for projects to succeed, staff work under pressure. While they may enjoy being innovative in the sheltered workshop, they seldom have time in their pressured daily grind to think conceptually, far less implement new ideas. Thus, a project's migration from theory to practice is not always smooth: prosaic operational reality is a whole other set of challenges beyond the sandbox. This is where we situate the skilled intermediary.

Learning to master intermediation practices can enrich the methods toolkit of media architecture practitioners. It equips the practitioner with the strategic vision and tactical acuity to broker their project's passage from idea to reality in difficult operational contexts. Design for mutual benefit, that is, benefit for all the actors in a scenario including gatekeepers, is a skill that goes beyond simply negotiating a project or artefact into the public realm. It positions the practitioner's imagination as a valuable enabler to a broader set of agendas: a navigator of complexity whose intervention can not only smooth the transition from theory to implementation but deliver benefits to others. The intermediary is a joiner of previously unseen dots, whose intervention adds practical, strategic and discursive value across diverse, sometimes divergent, fields of interest.

Method Steps ↗
https://mac2.mediaarchitecture.org/methods/intermediation

Annotated Portfolios

Communicating the qualities of media architecture through annotating and curating collections

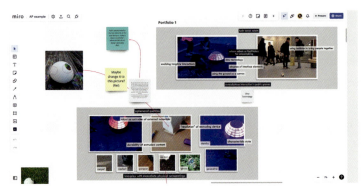

↑ Example annotated portfolio of two urban robotic artefacts. (Media credit: Marius Hoggenmüller.)

1 - Gaver, B., & Bowers, J. (2012). Annotated portfolios. *Interactions, 19*(4), 40–49.

Portfolios are widely used by design practitioners, including those who work in media architecture, to showcase their work in a curated format. They can incorporate images of the finished product or artwork, for example, a photograph of a media architecture installation taken on the opening night. Sometimes, designers also include drawings, renderings and photographs of early prototypes to illustrate their design process. Visual representations are often accompanied by a short summary text or brief textual annotations. Designers disseminate a portfolio in printed or digital form, such as a booklet or website. By containing a collection of works, it effectively communicates a designer's style, work processes and area of expertise.

Gaver and Bowers[1] first introduced the notion of annotated portfolios as a method to communicate design research. They allow design practitioners and researchers to articulate their work in a high-level and conceptual manner, while still maintaining a link to a particular design work. This is achieved by labelling the image of a project with short textual annotations, such as conceptual themes. A higher level of abstraction can also be reached by adding more projects to the portfolio. This can be exemplified by using some of the media architecture projects by the art and architecture studio realities:united as follows: the BIX Media Facade of the Kunsthaus Graz could be labelled with the conceptual theme 'building as a screen'.

The label 'fluorescent light rings' could be added to annotate the specific technology and lighting aesthetics of the facade. If other early media facade projects by realities:united are added to the portfolio, the label 'building as a screen' would still apply. The label 'fluorescent light rings', however, does not apply to some of the other facades that use LED technology. This label should be moved closer to the BIX Media Facade image, and a more high-level annotation like 'low-resolution media facade' or 'unconventional pixels' could be added.

A portfolio can be curated and labelled using different annotation strategies.[2] There is no specific rule for the type of annotations. However, a common strategy is to annotate about the design domain (e.g. 'building as a screen') or the qualities of interaction (e.g. 'playful interactions'). Another strategy is to organise and annotate a collection of works chronologically. Back to the realities:united project, a chronological order could demonstrate how their studio explored the larger design space of urban interaction over time, with some of the later projects exploring robotic elements rather than light-based media facades. As such, an annotated portfolio can not only communicate how a studio's work evolves over time but also how a community or field turns to new emerging technologies or engages with new topics.

Importantly, the original method has been proposed for design practitioners and researchers to annotate their own work. However, the method has evolved over the years, demonstrating the value of also annotating other people's work.[3] While not having first-hand insights, annotating other people's work can still be highly effective for visually traversing a design space and to facilitate design ideation.

Method Steps ↗
https://mac2.mediaarchitecture.org/methods/annotation

2 - Culén, A. L., Børsting, J., & Gaver, W. (2020, July). Strategies for Annotating Portfolios: Mapping Designs for New Domains. In *DIS '20: Proceedings of the 2020 ACM Designing Interactive Systems Conference*. Eindhoven, The Netherlands (1633–1645). Association for Computing Machinery.

3 - Hoggenmüller, M., Lee, W.-Y., Hespanhol, L., Jung, M., & Tomitsch, M. (2021, June). Eliciting New Perspectives in RtD Studies through Annotated Portfolios: A Case Study of Robotic Artefacts. In W. Ju, L. Oehlberg, S. Follmer, S. Fox, S. Kuznetsov. *DIS '21: Designing Interactive Systems Conference 2021,* Virtual Event, United States of America (1875–1886). Association for Computing Machinery.

Digital Storytelling
Making the media the message

The narratives created with digital media in media architecture play a key role in the entangled experience of mediated place. For the making of meaningful media experiences, digital storytelling (DST) presents a popular method. DST is a form of digital media production that enables personal narratives to be constructed, shared and digitally documented. While media artist Dana Atchley and Joe Lambert of StoryCenter are widely credited with the rise of DST, its popularity has surged due to the adaptation and appropriation of oral storytelling, where the radical and dynamic method of knowledge transmission has transcended to moving imagery, interactivity and non-linear storylines. DST is not as concerned with the sophistication of the imagery (such as in big budget movies) but places emphasis on the storyteller (what they choose to share and how they share it), as well as creativity in the production of the narratives. This allows for a range of storytellers beyond commercial filmmakers to tell personal, provocative and evocative stories.

Narrative, that is, when there is a clear beginning, a series of events and an ending to the story, is at the heart of DST. Narrative is a combination of description of the event(s) and providing the viewpoint of the narrator, as well as insight into the characters' thoughts and feelings within the event. A common narrative template is the hero's journey, where the hero goes through an adventure, comes to a crisis and then victoriously resolves the crisis (think *Lord of the Rings*!). Once a narrative has been identified, there are three key components of DST for media architecture: (1) the process of bringing the narrative to life through media architecture, i.e. ascertaining what media will support the narrative best, deciding how it will be created and gaining an understanding of the delivery environment; (2) the mediator i.e. individuals and teams who

↓ Lennon Wall which featured projections of support for Hong Kong's Umbrella Movement. (Media credit: Pasu Au Yeung, CC BY 2.0, via Wikimedia Commons)

work in collaboration with the storyteller to sequence create the media for digital displays, projections mixed reality environments; and (3) the eventual digital dia, which will include but not be limited to audio, vid- text, GIF and images. The making of the media can be achieved through a range of tools, such as digital cam- voice recorders, 3D software and virtual environment tools, such as Unity, Unreal Engine and smartphone apps. Due to this, DST offers a number of mediums, including digital videos, web-based stories, interac- stories and immersive experiences which include AR VR, artistic installations and computer games.

Given that DST can involve difficult and sen- sitive subjects, such as human rights abuses, DST diators often work towards reducing the risk of harm (such as vicarious trauma), insufficient attribution and compensation for storytellers and uninformed sent which can result in unethical making of sto- When care is taken in the making and displaying of it can have emancipatory effects for the storyteller and audience, build empathy and raise collective consciousness on social issues. Further, the con- of the media architecture needs to be understood, it ranges from an experience on a mobile phone large public digital screens. Thus, the mediator's role DST for media architecture needs to consider ethical dimensions, content curation, environment (public space, for example) and target audiences.

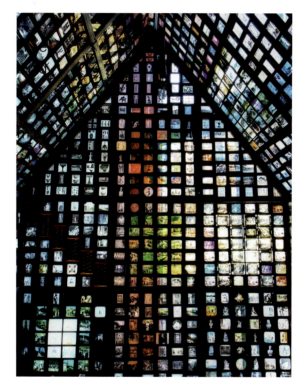

↑↑ The Van Gogh Exhibit: The Immersive Experience that celebrates the life and work of the expressionist artist Vincent van Gogh. (Media credit: 4nitsirk, CC BY-SA 2.0, via Wikimedia Commons.)

↑ The Lantern House, a Steve Tobin exhibit, composed of glass and antique slides used in 'magic lanterns', precursors to 35 mm slide projectors. (Media credit: Chris Costello, CC BY 2.0, via Flickr.)

Method Steps ↗
https://mac2.mediaarchitecture.org/methods/storytelling

Virtual Urban Prototyping

Design media architecture remotely and validate options before implementation

Prototyping a media architecture design solution, such as a digital facade, community LED wall or responsive sidewalk, means implementing enough of it to allow it to be tested by stakeholders and potential users. In doing so, designers can more confidently evaluate what it means to experience solutions in real life, and thus how appropriate they may be, reducing risks and costs of development and implementation. However, by its very nature, media architecture poses two big challenges to prototyping. First, it presupposes access to the target urban location and its infrastructure, which may not always be logistically practical, safe or even legally allowed before the solution reaches a certain level of maturity. Second, evaluating different options in situ may be too costly, particularly when comparing a range of choices for hardware, scale or placement of media within the city.

Virtual Urban Prototyping (VUP) involves the simulation, exclusively via software, of media architecture solutions for an urban space. Approaches can vary from the very simple to the highly sophisticated, depending on skills and resources available. In its simplest form, for example, it can be achieved merely with a photo or 2D digital representation of the target site, which can then be loaded as the background for an interactive code sketch—for example, in Processing or JavaScript—and overlaid with interactive graphics or animations. More advanced approaches may involve interactive 3D models of the media architecture, potentially accessible online. General steps include problem definition, platform selection, implementation, testing, analysis and recommendations.

The advantage of this approach is to enable the testing of interactions between humans and digital media in the built environment, which are often difficult to assess otherwise. As such, VUP can be highly useful for at least four reasons: (1) it allows specific elements of the solution to be tested, swapped, tweaked or combined in different ways without too much effort, in a safe and affordable way; (2) it can be particularly effective for identifying and eliminating unsuitable approaches early on in the project, thus helping narrow down the array of possible solutions; (3) it can assist with futureproofing a solution, by simulating options perhaps not yet entirely viable at present but which could eventually be scaled up; and (4) as the software can be distributed across members of a team, it allows for remote collaboration during design and testing. On the flip side, VUP's main drawback is that the user lacks the feeling of being immersed in the city, subject to all its spontaneous elements. As a result, VUP can only offer partial impressions into what the media architecture solution may actually feel like at the target site.

VUP should be used by urban interaction designers, product designers, artists, architects, urban planners or managers of media architecture projects. By offering a convenient way to 'mix and match' design elements and progressing through iterations of the design solution, VUP can be a powerful method to justify concepts, equipment and budget figures, as well as supporting decision-making, both prior to a proposal submission and during the early stages of design and development.

↑ Example of using a VUP before deploying the media architecture intervention. (Media credit: Luke Hespanhol)

Method Steps ↗
https://mac2.mediaarchitecture.org/methods/urban-prototyping

Spatial Prototyping
Exploring media architecture design by asking the right questions

1 - Rogers, Y., Marshall, P. & Carroll, J. (2017). *Research in the Wild*. Morgan & Claypool Publishers.

2 - Tomitsch, M., Wrigley, C., Borthwick, M., Ahmadpour, N., Frawley, J., Kocaballi, A., Núñez-Pacheco, C., Straker, K. & Loke, L. (2018). *Design. Think. Make. Break. Repeat: A Handbook of Methods* (1st ed.). BIS Publishers.

3 - Fatah gen. Schieck, A., Schnädelbach, H., Motta, W., Behrens, M., North, S., Ye, L. & Kostopoulou, E. (2014, June). Screens in the Wild: Exploring the Potential of Networked Urban Screens for Communities and Culture. In S. Gehring. *PerDis '14: Proceedings of The International Symposium on Pervasive Displays*. Copenhagen, Denmark (166–167). Association for Computing Machinery.

Interactions are situated in space and time. Situating media architecture within the city context requires a 'research-in-the-wild'[1]-driven methodology that tackles a complex range of spatial, temporal, socio-technical and aesthetic interactional considerations. The spatial prototyping method is similar to experience prototyping[2] but focuses on public experiences in real-world settings, which include the context of use, urban space inhabitants and passers-by. The method enables us to highlight the experiential dimensions: how people think, feel and act in situations with media architecture. It is a nested method that integrates approaches from architecture, anthropology, media art, interaction design and human-computer interaction.

Spatial prototyping uses an exploratory and iterative approach to integrate the hardware placement, media content development, local interactivity and distributed connectivity, creating situations and experiences that differ according to their local urban settings and the types of communities they support through different seasons.[3] This is achieved through exploring the questions of where, who, what and how? We can use any of these questions as a starting point for an investigation, before moving onto the next one. By going through the questions multiple times, it is possible to iteratively increase the fidelity of the solution.

For example, starting with the question of 'where?', we would identify suitable sites for the implementation. To develop a good understanding of how the built environment in these sites is currently structured, spatial analysis methods can be carried out, such as empirical observations, analysis in terms of visibility and accessibility, and social mapping of the groups and existing social practices—all of which are framed through the temporal aspect. The outcomes will inform the decisions regarding a range of locations suitable for the media installation placement.

Moving to the question of 'who?' involves mapping out the project stakeholders and collaborators (e.g. using the stakeholder mapping method), passers-by (single, groups, flows) and local communities and inhabitants. The results from this step inform the approach for engaging with local communities.

The question of 'what?' covers the technology (hardware, software) and its affordances (such as touch, touchless, computer vision, etc.).

The final question of 'how?' brings all steps together to frame the experience, media content development and interface creation of interactivity and connectivity. This can initially be tested as a real-scale mock-up in the lab with the research team, using other methods such as bodystorming and role-playing.[2] The effect of the placement in the urban context can be evaluated through observing behaviours before and after the implementation and capturing, periodically, emergent social interactions using observations and ethnographic methods.

The steps are repeated again, with a higher resolution and a more detailed approach, considering the learning from each step to feed into the next one.

Method Steps ↗
https://mac2.mediaarchitecture.org/methods/spatial-prototyping

Creating Interest
Beyond the launch of your media architecture intervention

Often, all the time and effort are spent on designing and building the media architecture intervention. But what happens after it is launched in the public sphere is in many ways even more important than the path towards that moment. This is the time when the public first sees the intervention, potentially on a large scale, which might be in terms of the intervention's size (e.g. if it is a media facade) or distribution (e.g. if it is a network of public screens).

Some of the authors of this book have experienced this firsthand with light installations exhibited as part of the Vivid Sydney festival. It is exhausting to get to the launch moment, but the real work, in terms of monitoring audience interaction, adjusting the content and maintaining its operation, lies on the other side of the launch. This experience is common to media facades and large urban screens. The developer makes sure the technology is installed according to the architect's specifications. But when the key is handed over, the platform only runs temporary placeholder content, and there is no plan in place for how it will maintain a connection to the local community. In the literature, this is referred to as the administration gap.[1]

Creating and maintaining interest involves a temporal staging sequence to manage expectations and to emphasise the value of iteration beyond the deployment of applications.[2] Depending on the context, this can be done through rolling out the media architecture intervention in stages, for example, testing it at a few locations before deploying it across an entire city or multiple cities. Whether the intervention spans multiple locations or not, clear signage provides a low-cost

↑ Countdown timer in Brisbane

1 - Lodato, T., & DiSalvo, C. (August, 2018). Institutional constraints: the forms and limits of participatory design in the public realm. *Proceedings of the 15th Participatory Design Conference: Full Papers - Volume 1,* Hasselt and Genk, Belgium (pp. 1–12). Association for Computing Machinery.

2 - Tomitsch, M. (2017). Making cities smarter. In *Making Cities Smarter*. JOVIS Verlag GmbH.

and effective way to communicate with the local public. This can include background information about the project: what the project aims to achieve; how long it will be in place for; whom to contact in case something isn't working or is broken; and, importantly, how people can get involved, which in its simplest form might just be through providing feedback.

For example, the City of Brisbane, Australia, used signage to inform people about the staged deployment of new countdown timers at traffic lights. The signs pointed passers-by to a website and a phone number where they could get more information. Ideally, such signage could include a call for participation or feedback with a QR code for people to directly connect via their smartphone.

↑ *Ampelpärchen* in Vienna

Doing this part of a project launch well contributes to the public acceptance of an intervention. In some cases, it may even lead to follow-up projects and deployments. For example, the city of Vienna, Austria, installed new pedestrian traffic light signals showing couples instead of the usual stick figures. The intervention was originally rolled out as a temporary installation at a few selected pedestrian crossings. However, it was strategically aligned to coincide with events happening in the city at the time, promoting tolerance and mutual respect. The initiative was featured so widely in global media that the city decided to continue the two-month deployment indefinitely and has since rolled out traffic light couples (*ampelpärchen*) at additional intersections.

Method Steps ↗
https://mac2.mediaarchitecture.org/methods/interest

Exploring Social Impact
An introduction to experiences, perceptions and change related to media architecture projects

Social impact assessment (SIA) is an established practice in many fields and a requirement for many policy, development and infrastructure projects. The goal is to understand how people experience change directly or indirectly because of a specific intervention and, when possible, alter a project to ensure positive change. SIA helps to assess if project objectives are achieved and to document other spin-off effects, whether intentional or unintentional, positive or negative. Evaluation can be speculative (anticipating future impacts of a project); formative (understanding impacts of project planning and construction as they occur); or summative (short- and long-term impacts of completed projects). Concerns in SIA—like community engagement and empowerment, sense of place and cultural heritage preservation—resonate with media architecture practices. For example, SIA could increase understanding of: the impacts of community consultation for local residents during the design process; how content resonates with audiences with different levels of media literacy; or the consequences of artistic and activist works for the people, places and issues they aim to address.

SIA prioritises human experience and wellbeing over other areas, such as economic or technological impacts. It is increasingly assessed in relation to environmental impacts, with some defining social impact as inclusive of changes to community and environment. Importantly, social change in this context is considered subjective—it refers to lived experiences, to how an intervention is felt or perceived. For the researcher, this requires an openness to different views of impact and the valuing of diverse voices and expertise. Stakeholders of media architecture projects might include creators, funders and target audiences, but their interpretations of impact provide only part of the picture and may conform to strategic priorities and existing indicators of success. Further exploration can reveal others affected beyond the immediate scope of the project, such as nearby residents (including non-humans) and business owners, passers-by or those responsible for the maintenance or decommissioning of an installation. One way to define social impact is in relation to scale and context. For example, the study could look at stakeholders of media architecture in a private, interior space, a certain neighbourhood, a local ecosystem or an international event.

There are a variety of approaches to evaluating social impact. For example, the Social Return on Investment (SROI) method[1] maps inputs (project resources), outputs (what the project does/creates) and outcomes (short- and medium-term changes resulting from the project) in order to understand the impacts (how changes affect people over time). By using money as a proxy for social value, SROI makes it easier to demonstrate and compare impacts where value has been difficult to quantify, particularly in community organisations. More recently, the UK Design Council[2] began developing methods to evaluate the social and environmental impacts of design projects. Their case study model invites practitioners to use qualitative (e.g. interviews, user stories) and quantitative (e.g. statistics, surveys) methods to assess the direct impacts of design projects as well as their 'invisible ripple effects.' Qualitative methods help to make sense of quantitative data and interpret social impact.

Understanding social impact requires a holistic view of the context and lifespan of a project. Acknowledging the experience and values of different stakeholders can help to ensure that project intentions reflect the priorities of the affected communities and increase positive social impacts.

Method Steps ↗
https://mac2.mediaarchitecture.org/methods/social-impact

↑ SIA project in Helsinki. (Media credit: Michel Nader Sayún.)

1 - Rogers, Y., Marshall, P. & Carroll, J. (2017). *Research in the Wild*. Morgan & Claypool Publishers.

2 - Tomitsch, M., Wrigley, C., Borthwick, M., Ahmadpour, N., Frawley, J., Kocaballi, A., Núñez-Pacheco, C., Straker, K. & Loke, L. (2018). *Design. Think. Make. Break. Repeat: A Handbook of Methods* (1st ed.). BIS Publishers.

The Practice section of the book is dedicated to documenting and showcasing the innovative and thought-provoking work being done in the field of media architecture. This section presents the 2018 and 2020 Media Architecture Award nominees and provides inspiration and guidance for future work in the field.

The section is organised around six award categories, each highlighting a different aspect of the discipline. The 'Animated Architecture' category showcases projects that creatively integrate digital media with buildings, typically in the form of media facades or large-scale media walls. The 'Money Architecture' category highlights projects that use media facades to represent economic status or create a sense of luxury and commercial interest.

The 'More-than-human Architecture' category recognises the importance of acknowledging the wellbeing of the natural ecosystem in the development of sustainable cities. The 'Participatory Architecture and Infrastructures' category highlights projects that allow participants to create or engage and interact with media content. The 'Spatial Media Art' category showcases experimental and avant-garde approaches to media art and its relationship with architecture.

Finally, the 'Future Trends and Prototypes' category highlights projects that reflect areas of growing attention and concern, such as climate change, carbon-neutral design, artificial intelligence and machine learning.

Through the examination of these award categories, the Practice section provides a comprehensive and diverse overview of the field of media architecture and its current state of development.

PRACTICE

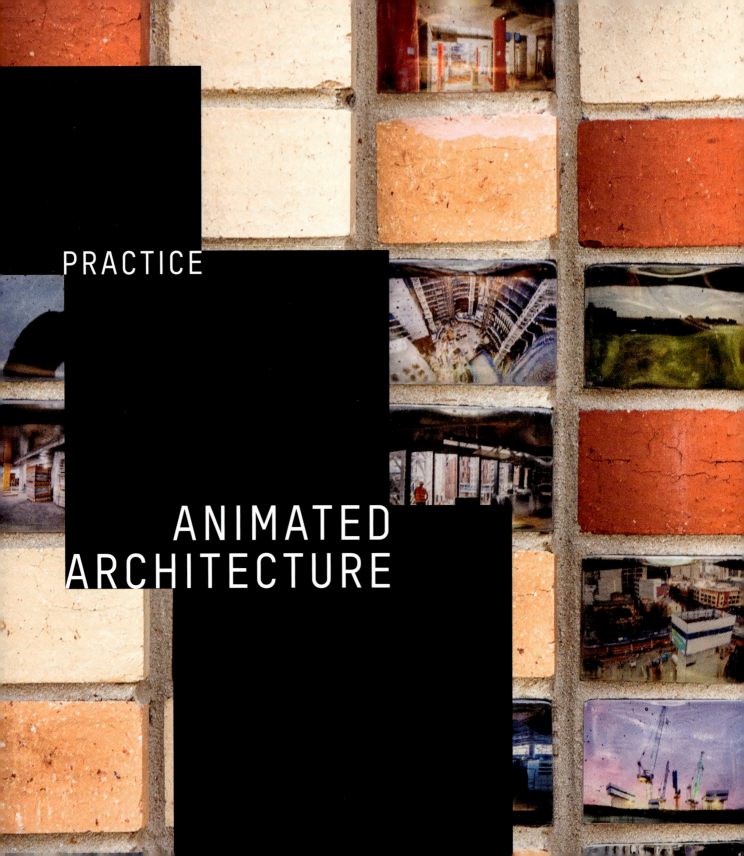

PRACTICE

ANIMATED ARCHITECTURE

The category Animated Architecture refers to projects that creatively integrate digital media with buildings, typically in the form of media facades or large-scale media walls. This intentional combination of dynamic media technologies with the built form creates a distinctive architectural medium.

Designers are increasingly focusing on the perception of the building, searching for designs that add layers of meaning and bring out new experiences of the building itself, the broader site and its surrounding public space. Although architecture has arguably played a vital role in communicating cultural, social, religious and political messages, now, with media facades, animated architecture is about representing 'communication' itself. This communication extends beyond the content portrayed on facades or building parts to include the public domain and building users as communicators, interactors, creators, players, contributors, collaborators, consumers or users.

The projects included in this section represent an array of approaches, methods, materials and technologies, demonstrating dynamic facades in diverse contexts, from interior airport lounges to public landmarks. They aim to create captivating visual experiences or interactive soundscapes that rely on the architecture as a framework, embodying the term Animated Architecture. With LED and interactive technologies becoming easier to program and more accessible, Animated Architecture has become a dominant form of architectural expression and communication in today's cities.

← The Digital Bricks, p.86. Image courtesy of Peter Casamento.

Changi Airport's Terminal 4 'Theatre of Experience'

↑1 ↗2
→3

Singapore
2017

Singapore's Changi Airport is constantly finding ways to transform the least appreciated travel moments into surprises of delight and discovery. Changi Airport Group commissioned Moment Factory to produce 'Theatre of Experience': two media features designed to entertain passengers as they navigate the airport. Using architectural media features that employ optical illusions and cinematic storytelling, the aim was to soothe the logistical aspects of the airport experience and captivate the audience in unique ways.

Passing through security screening, travellers are enveloped by an immersive media wall: The Panorama. In the heritage zone, real and virtual traditional shophouse facades create an authentic backdrop for local culture and storytelling. They become a whimsical 'stage' for a neighbourhood love story that brings two Peranakan families together.

The Panorama is a 70-metres-wide by 5-metres-tall LED screen, which displays seven panoramic content capsules. Each has a unique story and environment that transports the viewer's imagination to far-off places, allowing travellers to begin the journey before they are even through security. Picturesque high-altitude landscapes alternate with virtual bas-relief sculpture that subtly comes to life.

/ PRACTICE / ANIMATED ARCHITECTURE

The idea for 'Peranakan Love Story' was developed in collaboration with the iconic Singaporean singer Dick Lee and inspired by a row of traditional Peranakan shophouse facades being built inside the terminal, in the heritage zone. Using large format LED screens, 8 metres wide by 5 metres tall, and a *trompe-l'œil* approach to content, Moment Factory decided to bring one of the facades to life with a playful and local love story. While visitors shop and get something to eat, their mood is lightened by this touching story of two families coming together through a marriage—a tale that takes travellers on a journey deep into the heart of Singaporean culture.

Project Credits ↑ 4
Moment Factory
Dick Lee
Changi Airport Group (CAG)
SAA Architects Pte Ltd
Benoy
AECOM
Beca Carter Hollings & Ferner
Nanolumens

Media Credits
Moment Factory (1–6)

→ 5

→ 6

Kipnes Lantern

↑1 ↗2
→3

Ottawa, Canada
2017

A three-storey, hexagonal, glass tower of movement and light transforms and rejuvenates Ottawa's National Arts Centre. Launched in celebration of Canada's 150th anniversary, the Kipnes Lantern expands on the geometry of the original architecture, modernising it for the 21st century. Displayed content creates an aesthetic and unique digital experience that positively connects with members of the public.

The Lantern is a 15-metre-high transparent LED media facade, customised and designed by ClearLED and activated with visual content by Moment Factory. The transparent nature of The Lantern allows natural light to filter through while it displays distinct content during daylight or night-time—it is 80% transparent with a maximum brightness of 8000 nits. Content displayed on The Lantern can be coordinated with four additional 11-metre-high LED light blades on the main building.

Over 400 LED panels were customised and designed to fit each section of the glass building, with over 13 unique model types. All panels were individually fit- and quality-tested to mitigate problems during installation. ClearLED selected high-quality Nichia LEDs to ensure long-lasting light hours and to endure Ottawa's weather conditions.

This landmark beacon has become a canvas for digital artists to exhibit their work. Moment Factory's content framework provides a unique platform for the venue to showcase content from Canada and around the world, while bringing the National Art Centre's seasonal artistic program to life in an engaging and informative way. It is also a place to show off the National Art Centre's spirit and

← 4

sense of community: from screens designed to support World Mental Health Day to artworks that inspired hope and wellness during the difficult times of COVID-19 lockdowns. The Lantern and Blades is viewed by up to five million Ottawa residents and visitors to the capital per annum.

Project Credits
Oneoverchaos
Alex Doss
National Arts Centre, Ottawa
Diamond Schmitt Architects
Cleland Jardine Engineering
ClearLED
Moment Factory
Dr Dianne Kipnes and Mr Irving Kipnes

↑5 →6

Media Credits
ClearLED (2, 6)
Diamond Schmitt Architects (5)
Moment Factory (1, 3, 4)

77

MUURmelaar

Leuven, Belgium
2018

As passers-by meander around the curve of a building, away from the noises of the busy beltway into a quiet park, they are surprised and charmed by another sound entirely. MUURmelaar, a quirky translation of 'mumbling wall person', is an interactive media facade that translates people's behaviour into a dynamic soundscape of intriguing noises and rhythms. What was once a forgotten place, a banal pathway to be hurried down on the way to something else, is now deeply embedded in the social-cultural fabric of the neighbourhood as a place to discover, experiment and discuss.

When a passer-by encounters the facade, they are surprised by a soundscape which seemingly emanates from nowhere. The sounds and rhythms dynamically change according to the speed and direction of their movements. Casual passers-by stop, look around and inspect the facade, compelled to engage with the architecture. For local inhabitants and commuters, the pathway becomes a daily, playful route, as they test the hidden functionalities through trial and error and create new soundscapes.

The wooden windows of the DMOA office have been reinterpreted as architectural instruments. Each of the 17 window frames is equipped with a spring-actuated wooden block, which is agitated by an invisible and electronically controlled small physical hammer. A camera hidden in the roof registers the movements of anonymous passers-by. Their movements are analysed and translated into a playful sequence of sounds generated by the hammers touching the wooden blocks. Because it is dependent on the movements of the individual or individuals passing the building, the overall soundscape consists of unique and ever-changing combinations.

The architects decided not to include LEDs or light displays in the facade, as these would overpower the subtle material qualities. The dynamic media had to be invisible and unobtrusive, so that the wooden tones seem to be generated 'out of' the architecture itself.

Project Credits
Maarten Houben
Andrew Vande Moere
Benjamin Denef
Matthias Mattelaer
Research[x]Design at KU Leuven
DMOA Architects

Media Credits
DMOA Architects (3, 5)
KU Leuven (1, 2, 4)

↑1 →2

← 3

← 4

80   / PRACTICE / ANIMATED ARCHITECTURE

→ 5

DAZZLE | San Diego International Airport

↑ 1
→ 2

San Diego, United States of America
2017

Inspired by ship camouflage used in World War I, DAZZLE transforms the facade of the Rental Car Center of San Diego International Airport into a permanent media architecture artwork, visible to hundreds of thousands of motorists travelling past it daily on the adjacent freeway. DAZZLE was created using more than 2,000 tiles of a revolutionary material comparable to the technology used in handheld e-readers but modified for an architectural scale.

Artist team Ueberall International exploited the unique faceted half-kilometre-long facade of the Rental Car Center to create an animated landmark mural. The building displays custom, dynamic animations, which evoke water ripples, moving traffic, dancing snowflakes and shifting geometries.

To create this major visual impact, the artist team applied dazzle camouflage to the facade: a historic type of ship camouflage which hides objects in plain sight by visually scrambling their shapes and outlines—a phenomenon zebras and some wild cats use to disguise themselves in nature. After experimenting with different techniques to achieve this pattern, the team came up with the idea of applying e-paper technology to the facade, turning the building into a gigantic canvas that could display dynamic pixel animations.

DAZZLE is comprised of 2,100 autonomous E Ink Prism™ tiles, strategically placed wireless transmitters and a host computer. Each tile has a unique address to enable precise programming of countless visual patterns and is integrated with a photovoltaic cell for power, electronics for operation, and wireless communication. The activity of each tile is coordinated by the host computer, with information transmitted through Ethernet wires to wireless transmitters that face the building. The wireless transmitters forward the information to clusters of tiles, which then forward the data on to further tiles. Based on these instructions the individual tiles will transition from black to white.

Project Credits
Nik Hafermaas
Dan Goods
David Delgado
Jeano Erforth
Ivan Cruz
San Diego International Airport Art Commission
Ueberall International
E Ink Corporation

Media Credits
Pablo Mason (2, 3, 4, 5)
Ricky Williams (1)

↑↑ 3
↑ 4

The Digital Bricks

↑1 ↗2

Melbourne, Australia
2021

For centuries, clay bricks have shaped the appearance, feeling and expression of the built environment. Inspired by this traditional building material, The Digital Bricks fuses technology and architecture with First Nations Australians' culture. Polished, translucent glass bricks and high-definition screen technology interlace with clay brickwork to manifest the concept 'if these walls could talk' and share stories of scientific innovation, First Australians' knowledge, and art programs through the touch responsive media facade.

Melbourne Connect, the newly built innovation precinct at The University of Melbourne, celebrates traditional material by intertwining its physical and tactile strengths with the opportunities afforded by today's digital and interactive technologies. Science Gallery Melbourne sits at the

86 / PRACTICE / ANIMATED ARCHITECTURE

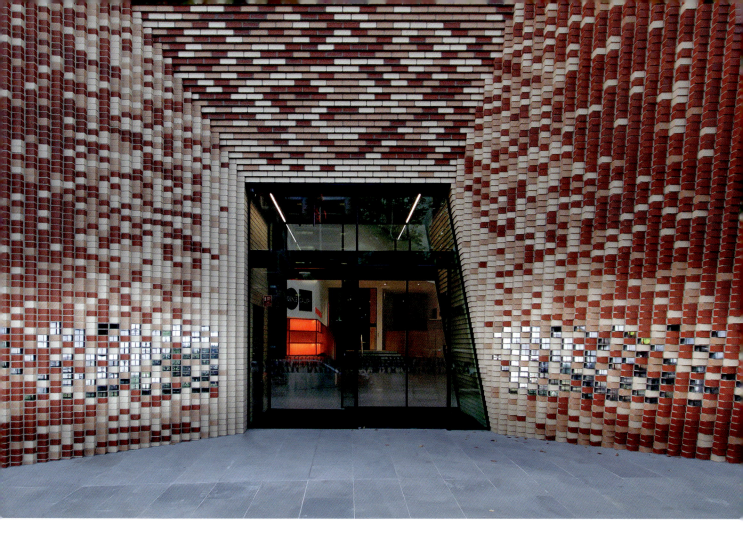

gateway to this precinct, with The Digital Bricks a perfect platform to share stories from its rich history. The debut content program consists of *The Digital Birthing Tree*, a First Australians-led program that displays gradual transitions from pre-colonial knowledge to Western colonisation and occupation of Traditional Lands. The story provides an opportunity to honour First Australian Women's contributions to the health system.

The Digital Bricks incorporates interlaced placement of 226 polished translucent glass bricks within the building's clay brick ground floor structure. Each glass brick sits in front of a small, high-brightness and high-resolution LED screen. This transparent mosaic of so-called 'digital bricks' are placed strategically by way of a parametric model that feathers glass bricks with clay bricks to ensure optimal visibility.

The technology behind The Digital Bricks results from design research by the Science Gallery Melbourne and the School of Computing and Information Systems, in partnership with Melbourne Connect. At 208 physical megapixels it was the world's highest resolution interactive video screen at the time it was built. The project's complexity necessitated significant innovations and developments across all disciplines. For example, facade engineers and building teams had to invent new ways to bond clay and glass bricks and reliable methods to embed the screens in wall cavities.

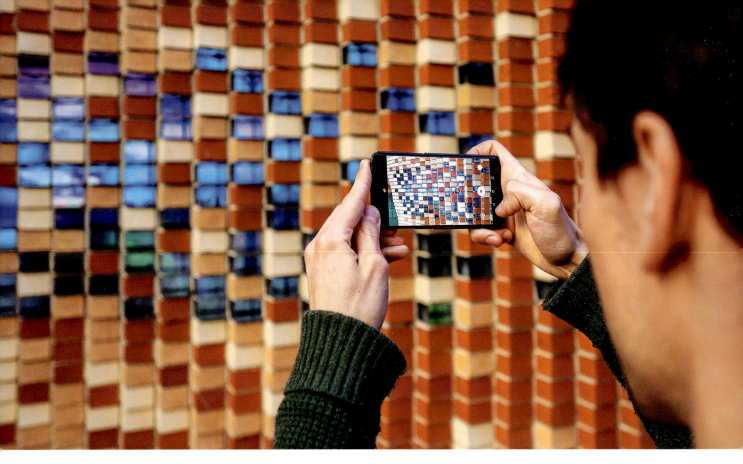

Project Credits ↑ 3
Science Gallery Melbourne ← 4
Arup
The University of Melbourne
Melbourne Connect
Woods Bagot
Byrne Construction Systems
AVIT Integration
REELIZE.STUDIO
Light-Ctrl
Lendlease

Media Credits
Peter Casamento (1)
Toby Welch (3, 4)
Niels Wouters (2, 5, 6)

→ 5

→ 6
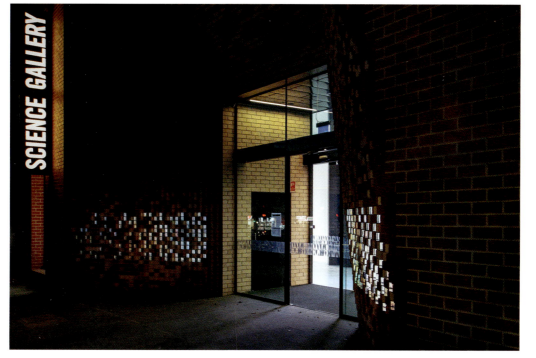

Window into the Seas

Bremerhaven, Germany
2020

After dark, a ship-sized landmark made of light frames the exhibits of a maritime museum. The interior is illuminated, so it can be viewed from afar, even when the museum itself is closed. This is light on an immense scale; it fills the view. You can even walk inside its confines, framed by ripples of glowing colour.

Window into the Seas combines exhibits and multi-media projections to showcase maritime questions of relevance to society. The German Maritime Museum/ Leibniz Institute for Maritime Museum is located in Bremerhaven's Old Harbour, providing a direct connection to the city's maritime history. For the 30th anniversary of German unification, Xenorama developed an immersive show emanating from a tidal calculator—a mechanical computer used to predict ebb and flow—manufactured in East Germany in 1955. The content spanned the entire facade of the museum and connected the interior projection surfaces to an outer LED frame.

The 75-metres-wide and 6.3-metres-high media facade is made up of three elements: the FRAME, the projectors and the speakers. The FRAME is a permanent light installation conceptualised by Helmut M. Bien, designed by Dirk Mailänder and implemented by LightLife. 98 iGuzzini Linealuce Mini 47 LED-bars illuminate the concrete window frame of the museum. Within the building, the projectors and sound-equipment setup—designed by Xenorama—is positioned to allow synchronisation between the projections and the FRAME's light display.

→ 2

The project connects the museum's interior exhibition space with the surrounding public grounds, allowing it to blend into the night view of Bremerhaven. Researchers and new media artists collaborate to translate scientific content into a powerful and memorable audiovisual experience that is easily accessible for a broad audience.

Project Credits
German Maritime Museum –
    Exhibition Department
Leibniz Institute for Maritime History
Dietrich Bangert
Westermann Kommunikation
Helmut M. Bien & mailänder licht design
Dirk Mailänder
LightLife –
    Lukas Gössling, Antonius Quodt
Xenorama –
    Marcel Bückner, Tim Heinze, Richard Oeckel,
    Lorenz Potthast, Moritz Richartz
Pharos
Christoph Geiger
vvvv
Die Senatorin für Wissenschaft und Häfen –
    Freie Hansestadt Bremen Leibniz
    Research Museums
Hochschule für Künste Bremen –
    Prof. Roland Lambrette
Hergarten –
    Interactive Environments, Hamburg

Media Credits
DSM / Hauke Dressler (1, 2, 5, 6, 7)
Xenorama (3, 4)

↑↑↑ 3
↑↑ 4
↑ 5

→ 6

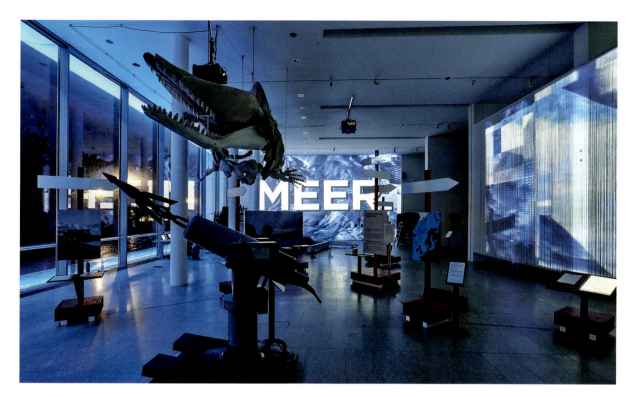

→ 7

93

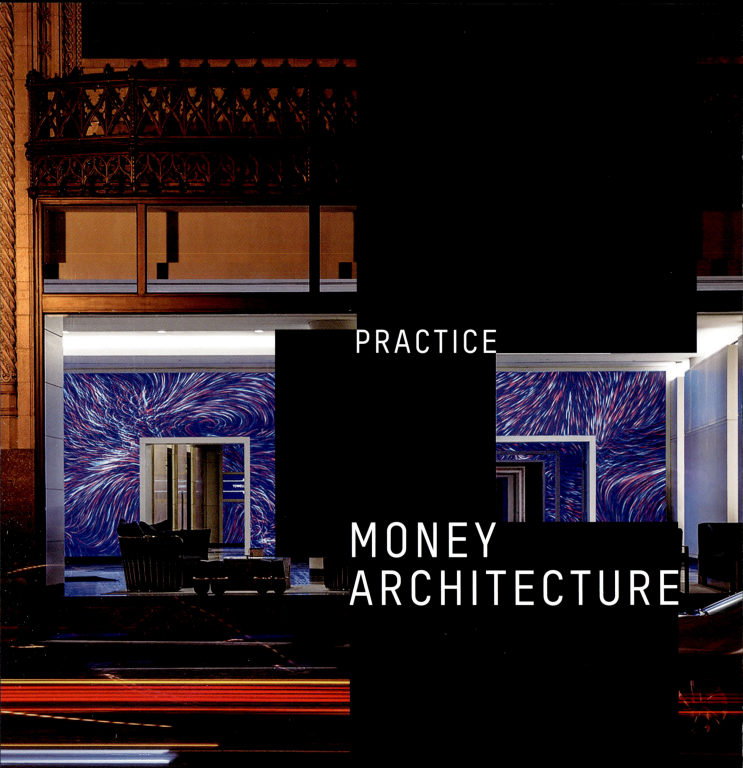

PRACTICE

MONEY
ARCHITECTURE

Money Architecture as a category incorporates projects using media facades to represent economic status or create a sense of luxury and commercial interest. Often these projects are commissioned by banks, insurance companies, shopping centres or casinos. These projects have a tendency to employ media facades to entice or attract people or to convey messages related to the products they sell for financial gain.

The media facades are not limited to exterior parts of the buildings with many public buildings and shopping centres using large-format and high-resolution LED screens as the basis for their interior design. Customers are engaged in experiences that transport them from the reality of their day-to-day lives, allowing them to envision and experience opulent, artistic or natural settings.

The projects in this section reflect a growing trend where companies are using different means to connect customers with the innovations of their products, such as new material and technological developments or the company's ethical principles. There has recently been a shift to address sustainability-related concerns, raise awareness of natural environments and create a sense of place through media facades, interactive screens and sound installations. As such, the Media Architecture Biennale 2018 was the last competition to award projects in this category.

← Terrell Place, p. 104. Image courtesy of Caleb Tkach.

↑1

Hyundai Pavilion Interactive Water Installation

Pyeongchang, South Korea
2018

Entering a dark structure pinpricked with light, visitors encountered a vast white 'water' room, with 25,000 singular water droplets slipping along grooved trails every minute. These droplets were inspired by hydrogen molecules: the technology behind Hyundai's hydrogen fuel cell vehicle. Visitors interacted with the multi-sensory installation via a series of haptic sensors to create new rhythms as droplets continually collided, joined and split across the water landscape.

↑ 2

Hyundai Motor commissioned the 35 by 35-metres pavilion for the Pyeongchang Winter Olympics 2018 in South Korea. It was located at a central site in the Olympic Park and attracted a total of 60,000 visitors. The water installation, consisting of a three-dimensionally curved Corian surface, extended over nearly the entire area of the 20 by 12-metres space. Water grooves interacted in complicated ways, including intersections, splits and junctions. A total of 258 nozzles were built into the circumference; these could be switched on and off, and the size and frequency of the droplets could be manually adjusted.

The entire surface of the installation was finished with a hydrophobic coating, so the water droplets could remain intact and run at an unnaturally fast speed towards a basin at the lower end. As the individual droplets collected, a 'lake' grew at the lowest point, draining and reappearing every few minutes.

↑ 3

Visitors were given the opportunity to interact in two ways. By pouring water into a small funnel on the edge of the installation, they could stop a large part of the water flow, with only the valve directly under the funnel remaining open. A second interaction involved sensors that reacted to the physical proximity of visitors. As they moved their hands over a small aperture emitting a gentle draft of air, the rhythm of water droplets emerging from the valve beneath doubled in speed.

Project Credits
Asif Khan
iart
Hyundai Motor Company
Cutting Edge
Institute of Thermal and Fluid Engineering FHNW
Innocean Worldwide

Media Credits
Luke Hayes (1–4)

↑1

Firefly

Paris, France
2017

As sunset arrives, a lush green facade comes alive. At first, a single, tiny light blinks on, then another and another. The fireflies are waking up. It begins slowly, but soon they start to communicate, until the whole building shimmers with light. Passers-by suddenly realise that this is not just decorative lighting; these are man-made fireflies. They are witnessing an exciting fusion of nature and technology.

The living facade of La Grande Épicerie de Paris' fine grocery store has transformed the neighbourhood of the 16th *arrondissement's* urban landscape to reconnect the public with the positivity and joy that the natural world evokes. Nature returns to the city with a green wall of aromatic plants used in cooking and herbalism, mixed in with perennials and grasses. Rather than only creating a pleasing aesthetic, the facade has important functionality: it absorbs noise, filters and fertilises the air, and cools down the building during the summer months.

↑ 2

The living wall was created using pre-planted boxes that are attached vertically. The luminaires are installed between these to create the firefly effect. LED fixtures use a customised optical system to display the light in front of the plants. The optic creates a very small direct light (the 'firefly') and an indirect glow by reflecting most of the light back onto the plants. Dimming the light decreases the size of the glow to make it seem as though fireflies are hovering around the facade.

The 500 LED fixtures are installed in a random pattern, with a distance of 50–150 centimetres, and can be controlled separately. They use warm white light combined with green and red to enhance the colour of the plants. Cabling is mounted in a way to protect it during plant maintenance and pruning, with four different length lights to maintain a random pattern despite changes in vegetation depth.

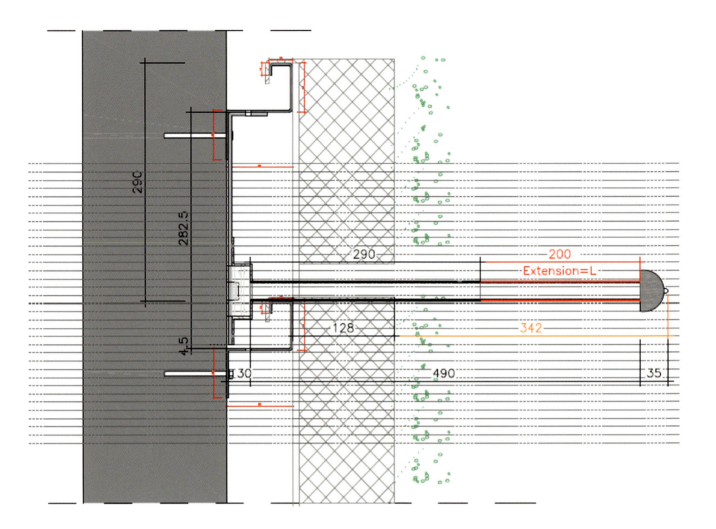

↑ 3

Project Credits
La Grande Épicerie de Paris
FRANCK ET FILS
Tracer Urban Nature
Tiphaine Treins
Temeloy
Andreas Barthelmes
LightLife
Osram

Media Credits
Lightlife (3)
Kaixin Lyu (1, 2, 4, 5)

→ 4

→ 5

103

Terrell Place

Washington, D.C., United States of America
2016

Even if you arrive at the lobby of Terrell Place at the same time every day, it will always be a different experience. 158 square metres of motion-activated LED displays create an ever-evolving responsive artwork that reacts to the presence of people; the walls move with you.

When Beacon Capital Partners acquired Terrell Place—where civil rights activist Mary Church Terrell once led a protest against segregation—they tasked ESI Design with creating a more harmonious interior and a contemporary, exciting work destination. In the first month after its launch, Terrell Place became an internet sensation, with more than 75 million views on social media, and a must-see destination for both locals and tourists. At 25 metres wide and 4 metres high, the largest media wall captures the attention and curiosity of passers-by, who can see it through the oversized windows.

↑ 2

To create a strong sense of connection across two reception areas and the hallway leading between them, the space was treated as a single media canvas. Activated by infrared sensor technology, the LED screens respond to the motion of people walking or standing still, creating scenes that ebb and flow with the morning rush and the afternoon lull. Three beautiful custom content modes play with varying durations and sequences, ensuring that visitors never see the same scene twice: 'Seasons'—showing the life cycle of Washington, D.C.'s cherry blossoms; 'Color Play'—displaying algorithmically generated patterns of multicoloured threads; and 'City Scape'—a homage to the city with iconic architecture, statuary and transportation scenes.

Lighting, sound and media were designed to deliver a cohesive multimodal experience. Some lights change colour and temperature according to the media that is playing. Ambient sounds emerge from invisible speakers in the walls and ceiling, creating a fully immersive experience.

↑ 3

Project Credits
ESI Design
Beacon Capital Partners
Gensler
Advance Structural Concept LLC
Art Display Co.
Diversified Systems
VER
AV&C
Cinematic Interiors
30/70 Productions Ltd.

Media Credits
Caleb Tkach (1–4)

106 / PRACTICE / MONEY ARCHITECTURE

↑ 4

PRACTICE

MORE
THAN
HUMAN
ARCHITECTURE

To achieve sustainable cities, media architecture needs to embrace the wellbeing of the natural ecosystem as a whole and go beyond the needs of only humans. It is essential to acknowledge that the planet is rapidly becoming more urbanised and that natural environments are becoming compromised and encapsulated in increasing urban areas. Severe strain is placed on animals, plants, insects and the broader ecosystem, impacting the health of all living beings on our planet.

At the Media Architecture Biennale 2020 the category of More-than-human Architecture was added to the media architecture awards as a step towards recognising the efforts made by designers, through media architecture, to create better awareness of the impact humans have on this planet. This acknowledges the critical role that media architecture can play to enable a 'live together' approach with other beings in ways that respect their needs and can support their wellbeing.

The projects included in the More-than-human Architecture category employ digital technologies to raise awareness about ecological, sustainable urban futures and to help consider non-human actors and perspectives, which include natural and artificial life forms.

← Aukio, p. 110. Image courtesy of Rune & Berg.

Aukio

Helsinki, Finland
2019

Imagine you could step off a long, cramped flight straight into the magic of a forest or a snowscape with the northern lights dancing above. This is the healing experience of Aukio, an immersive interactive journey right in the heart of Helsinki Airport. For some passengers this will be their first, or perhaps their only, impression of Finland: state-of-the-art technology and the beauty of Finnish nature.

Digital elements were used to imitate nature as it is; pure, magical and full of wonders. The immersive experience of Aukio was created in a 400-square-metres, triangular, two-storey plaza with a wavy 75-metres-long curved LED surface surrounding it. High-quality 4 x 8 K 360° videos are projected onto the surface, with the experience intensified by spatial sound and interactive wooden walls.

Passengers can encounter all four seasons of the Finnish year cycle, showing different times of day: altogether there are 16 varying landscapes. Aukio can delight passengers with a polar night lit by the aurora, flowers blooming on a spring dawn or the reds and gold of an autumn evening. By touching the birch-panelled walls, passengers can also interact with the landscape: the space responds to them by generating nature-imitating audiovisual animations, such as luminous northern lights or swirling autumn leaves. All of this creates a profound connection to the surrounding landscape, as well as magical moments for kids and the playful-minded. Visitors can also explore facts about the different landscapes, natural phenomena, and Finns and their relationship with nature.

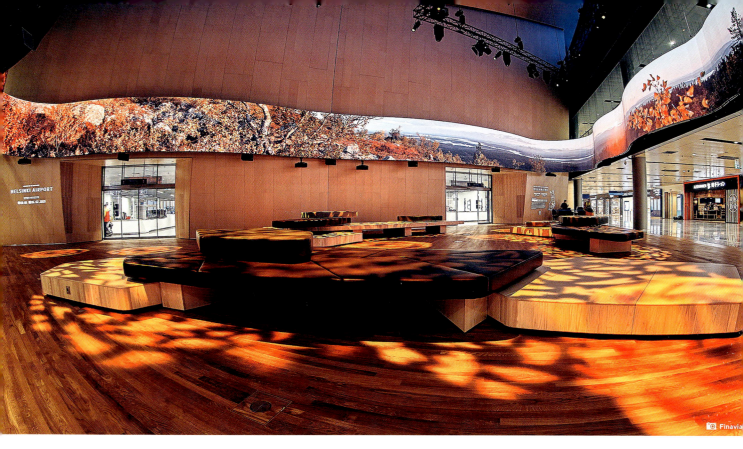

All humans experience a connection with nature that affects us in conscious and unconscious ways. In a space that is essentially distanced from nature—the built-up environment of an airport—the creators of Aukio recognised the need for meaningful digital and spatial experiences that can re-establish this connection to create a sense of well-being and relaxation.

Project Credits
OiOi Collective
Granlund
Architects Davidsson Tarkela
Rune & Berg Design
Finavia—Helsinki Airport
PES-Architects
Studiotec
Flatlight Creative
Christie Pandoras Box

Media Credits
Finavia (1, 2, 4, 5)
Flatlight Creative (6, 7)
Rune & Berg (3)

↖1 ↑↑2
↑3

111

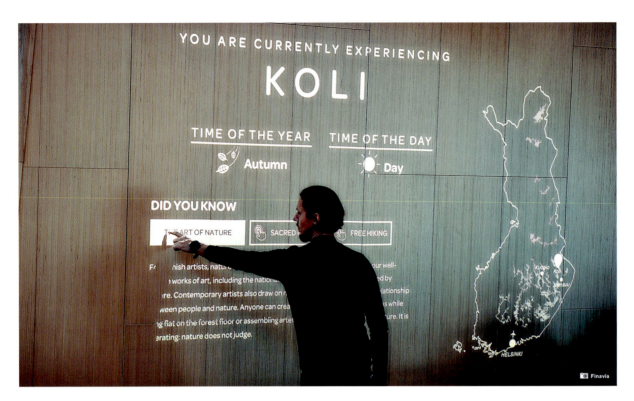

← 4

← 5

112 / PRACTICE / MORE-THAN-HUMAN ARCHITECTURE

→ 6

→ 7

113

GROW

Rotterdam, The Netherlands
2020

Most of the time, we scarcely notice the large tracts of land that are responsible for feeding us. We look upon these fields as vacant, empty and uninhabited, and yet they are teeming with the life that sustains us. GROW was designed to bring an awareness of the beauty of agriculture by turning an enormous field into a luminous dreamscape of red and blue waves of light.

Inspired by scientific light recipes that improve the growth and resilience of plants, Daan Roosegaarde and his team sought to answer important questions of agricultural innovation: how can cutting-edge light design help plants grow more sustainably; how can we make the farmer the hero? The poetic 'dancing light' effect of GROW was created using a design-based light 'recipe' which shines across 20,000 square metres of farmland growing leek. Light science technology in photobiology has found that certain combinations of blue, red and ultraviolet light can enhance plant growth and reduce the use of pesticides by up to 50%. The light display was created using four systems of light recipes on solar batteries. Precision lightning was focussed horizontally across a controlled area, which extended the effect of the sunlight for a short time. The installation could only be seen from nearby to avoid light pollution.

GROW was created as part of the artist-in-residence program of Rabobank and is the first in a series of dreamscapes by Studio Roosegaarde, which show the beauty of combining art and science to create a better world. GROW helps us understand how light can benefit plants, but it is also a call for enlightenment during these dark times—to send out a hopeful light when people need it most. By reframing the landscape as a living cultural artwork, GROW also gives a new meaning to the word 'agri-culture'.

Project Credits
Daan Roosegaarde
Studio Roosegaarde
Rabobank

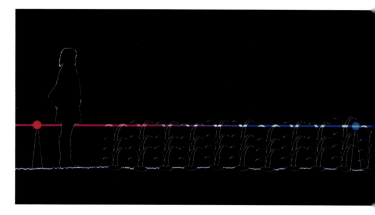

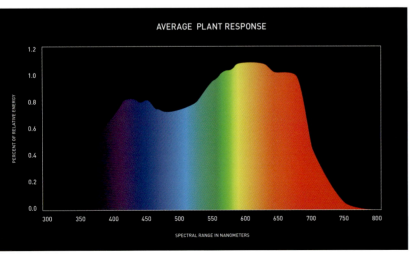

Media Credits
Studio Roosegaarde (1-9)

↑ 3

← 4

↖5 ↑6
←7

↙8 ↓9

Touching Night Skies
50°06'44"N 8°40'36"E

Frankfurt am Main, Germany
2020

In the shadow of the brightest high-rises in Germany, you enter a dark corridor. Black walls surround you, so that after a few steps, you can no longer see the city at all. The space around you has 'disappeared'—corners and edges are invisible. All that remains is the bright night sky above and the certainty of both feet standing on the city pavement. This is 'darkness' within a city teeming with lights.

As cities become denser and brighter with light pollution, the night sky is a casualty. To view the stars, so long an inspiration for the Romantic artists, one must seek out the remotest corners of Germany. But there is also a modern romanticism to the illuminated skyline. Touching Night Skies sought to address this contradiction: a temporary art installation that brought the immersive experience of 'darkness' into a highly illuminated urban setting. The installation was created for the Luminale festival in Frankfurt am Main, a city with one of the brightest night skies in Germany. Touching Night Skies was constructed at the Roßmarkt central square, directly below the high-rises of downtown, at the precise location 50°06'44"N 8°40'36"E.

Two angled wall elements interlocked to create a small courtyard with no roof. When inside, surrounding buildings were no longer visible—the only view was up towards a patch of night sky. The walls were painted with the blackest paint available, which robbed all surfaces of their material properties and made it impossible to perceive corners. This created an ambiguous space where the 'room' became absent, and the focus was on the contrast between the black paint and the bright night sky.

↑ 3

Touching Night Skies addressed the conflict at the heart of our contemporary understanding of urban lighting design and desire for night-time security: the issue of light pollution in a world where LED technology is becoming more prevalent.

Project Credits
Tobias Ziegler—TBSZGLR
Christof Grumpelt
Flo Service
Luminale e.V.
Messe Frankfurt

Media Credits
TBSZGLR / C. Grumpelt (1–4)

↑ 4

PRACTICE

PARTICIPATORY ARCHITECTURE AND INFRASTRUCTURES

Participatory Architecture and Infrastructures projects allow participants to create or engage and interact with media content. Often the content provides a means for participants to connect to or communicate with one another to address issues of social marginalisation and inclusion or to promote civil rights and action. These projects aim to impact social and political life in the city and empower citizens to become active participants in their communities. Designers of these projects explore design processes, interaction modalities and platforms to allow for diverse input methods and media and to encourage participation from across a cities' population and urban infrastructures. These projects consist of hybrid systems with both digital and physical components.

Projects in this category tend to be complex in their creative combination of physical and digital materials with new technologies and media forms. In some instances projects are of a large scale, spreading across a city via festival formats or using projection to cover entire building facades, while other projects are subtle and place specific. Concepts and theories from placemaking, play and co-design tend to drive the design approaches of many Participatory Architecture and Infrastructure projects, with the common thread being the intention of participation of others in the projects.

← ARENA, p. 124. Image courtesy of B. Maubrey.

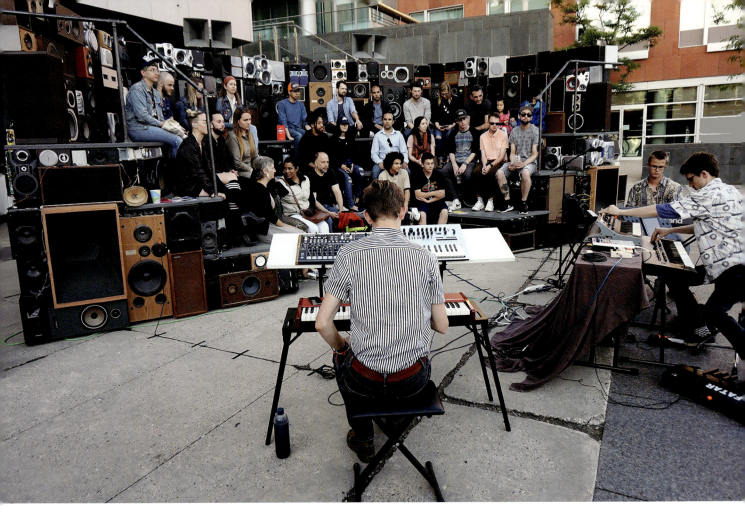

↑1

ARENA

Kitchener, Canada
2018

ARENA is a challenge to the public to make noise and be heard. It is an amphitheatre constructed with 320 recycled loudspeakers that brings people together to share their music and thoughts. The speakers that make up the installation represent years of sound technology and were acquired from all sorts of places: thrift shops, junk stores—they were donated by friends and supporters, but also by complete strangers who just wanted to clean out their basements.

ARENA is a mobile, interactive sound sculpture by Berlin-based artist Benoît Maubrey. It was constructed at Lot 42, a former steel factory in Kitchener, and debuted at the True North technology conference in Waterloo, after which it was installed in Carl Zehr Square at the Kitchener City Hall during the CAFKA biennale in 2018. The sculpture won first prize at the Hacking Urban Furniture contest in 2017.

↑2

The public, local artists, musicians, choral groups and organisations can relay songs and messages to the speakers in three ways: via Bluetooth and individual smartphones; by calling a telephone number with an automatic answering service; or by using the available microphone or connecting their devices and instruments by plugging them into the line in jacks. All the speakers are connected to two amplifiers and a mixing board. Volume can be controlled via the mixing board, with individual amplifiers and receivers situated in a small storage space nearby. The sculpture is constructed as four sections, which can be transported using a 33' flatbed truck.

The sculpture becomes a mobile 'Speakers Corner'—a hotspot for local participation and self-expression, as well as a stage for small events and concerts. ARENA is also a visual reminder of the value that recycled objects and e-waste can still hold.

↑ 3

Project Credits
Benoît Maubrey
Jan Fuhrmann
Rex Lingwood
Jago Whitehead
Gordon Hatt
Johnny Camara
CAFKA, Kitchener Canada

Media Credits
Lea Clarin (1–3, 5)
B. Maubrey (4)

126 / PRACTICE / PARTICIPATORY ARCHITECTURE AND INFRASTRUCTURES

↑ 4   → 5

↑1

Chave do Centro
'The Key to Downtown'

São Paulo, Brazil
2017

Can art be used as a tool to facilitate urban restoration and change how people interact with the city? This question was at the heart of Chave do Centro, a 30-night-long media facade festival with the aim of attracting pedestrians to a long overpass that had destroyed urban cohesion in downtown São Paulo.

During the military dictatorship in Brazil, in the 1960s, a three-kilometres-long overpass was built in downtown São Paulo to speed up traffic between the east and west side of town. As a side effect the whole of downtown suffered urban decay; noise and pollution increased tenfold in the areas around the overpass. Traffic was allowed 24 hours a day. The neighbourhood became an unsafe place to walk, particularly at night.

↑ 2

Though Democracy came back in the 1980s, it has taken more than 35 years for residents of the neighbourhood to succeed in a campaign to decrease the opening hours of the overpass—the *Minhocão*, or the 'Big Worm', a nickname given to it by residents—and to open it for pedestrians. Artist and producer Alexis Anastasiou, a local resident, created Chave do Centro, a media art festival that placed four installations from different artists at locations along the overpass best viewed from a walk along it.

Images were projected onto non-treated, standard brick buildings. Media servers and laser projectors were placed inside peoples' homes, to achieve the low cost necessary to have projections running for 30 nights.

↑ 3

The festival was a great success, attracting lots of visitors and media attention, and helping raise awareness about the importance of art and a good environment for pedestrians. Shortly after the festival concluded, the City Council approved longer hours for pedestrians—now the overpass is only open for cars on weekdays from 7 am to 8 pm and is officially called the 'Minhocão Park'.

Project Credits
Alexis Anastasiou
Roberta Carvalho
VJ Vigas
Felipe Mororzini
Visualfarm
Thales Augusto
Christie Pandoras Box
Resolume
Miguel Adianio e Sergio Cordoba
EPSON

Media Credits
Cleber Portaro (3-4)
visualfarm diagram (2)
Joao Vitor Grassi (1)

↑1 →2

Digital Calligraffiti

Berlin, Germany
2017

In a time when our language is almost exclusively digital, what messages do we wish to 'write beautifully' and pass on? Digital Calligraffiti is a new form of intercultural exchange that combines the traditional art forms of calligraphy and graffiti with responsive urban media art. It was initially developed to give young refugees living in Berlin a public stage to share their messages and views on current topics, using the urban screens and walls of the city as their canvas in a real-time performance.

Digital Calligraffiti is a community project and artistic campaign that endeavours to contribute to the integration of migrating cultures. Representatives of these cultures were invited to the 'Digital Calligraffiti Camp' to work together with traditional calligraphers and calligraffiti and

↑ 3

urban media artists to investigate questions of sharing values, for instance, what cultural values do people with migration backgrounds wish to preserve from decaying and integrate into their lives today? In a co-design process, the participants from migrating cultures learned how to draw calligraffiti and animate the analogue creation of their artworks using digital infrastructure.

Artworks were created using Infl3tor: an interactive light table that enabled live visualisation of the ideas and emotions of the participants. Infl3tor was especially designed for Digital Calligraffiti by media artists Michael Ang and Hamza Abu Ayyash and can also facilitate a translocal dialogue beyond physical borders. The written statements from two cities, in the initial instance Berlin and Durban, can 'meet' on the projection wall or screen and are visualised through different colours.

The participatory projection format gives all social groups a chance to freely share their wishes and visions, co-created with the artistic guidance of renowned calligraffiti artists. In a time where the transportation of refugees is a burning matter, this project opens up new avenues of communication, empowering, at least, the transportation of thoughts.

↑ 4

Project Credits
Public Art Lab
From Home to Fame Publishing
Michael Ang
Hamza Abu Ayyash
Michael Ang
Calligraffiti Artists
European Union
Creative Europe Program

Media Credits
Ruthe Zuntz (1–4)

↑1

ANTopolis

Linz, Austria
2020

For three evenings in 2020, virtual ants invaded the city of Linz. The city became an ANTopolis, a nest of artificial ants seeking out human activities. They crawled towards man-made shapes, organising themselves to create images of people, vehicles and buildings. Both the moving and still parts of the city became their resource.

During the Ars Electronica Festival in 2020, passers-by in the Hauptplatz (main square) of Linz were welcomed to participate in the interactive media facade project ANTopolis and become part of the artwork by allowing the artificial ants to create a portrait of them. The participant stood in front of a camera, and their likeness was captured in the shapes and trails made by thousands of ants, creating a unique and constantly moving image of the human face. This image was projected onto a giant screen above the square.

↑2 ↑3

ANTopolis was projected onto the main facade of the University of Art and Design Linz, using a 16 by 9 metres front projection screen. The artwork can also be displayed directly onto a facade. A camera transmits the image of a person standing in front of it wirelessly to a computer. The picture is then transformed into a drawing using contrast zones, forming trails which each virtual ant is then free to follow and creating a real-time portrait of the participant. As soon as the person moves a little, the ants scatter and the picture changes.

Tiny things can still have a big impact on human activities, whether it is a microscopic virus—that was able to bring human activity to an almost complete standstill—or a miniscule insect. ANTopolis seeks to remind us that we are not an immune and independent entity who can keep exploiting natural resources; we are only one part of a large and fragile ecosystem.

Project Credits
Laurent Mignonneau
Christa Sommerer
Kunstuniversität Linz
Ton & Bild Medientechnik Gmbh
Manuela Naveau

Media Credits
Laurent Mignonneau & Christa Sommerer (1-7)

← 4

← 5

← 6

→ 7

↑1

Citizen Dialog Kit

Leuven, Genk, Houthalen-Helchteren, Peer, Antwerp,
Heist-op-den-Berg, Ghent; Belgium
Amsterdam, The Netherlands
2019

How can you make the public part of the conversation at the location where it matters? Citizen Dialog Kit is an interactive and wireless display toolkit that is designed to facilitate communication between citizens and civic organisations. This easy to deploy media architectural interface is flexible to install and encourages dialogues with a broad range of people through playful interactions.

Citizen Dialog Kit's interactive display devices allow civic stakeholders to inform and survey passers-by in a public space. Organisations can pose responsive questions that change depending on previous answers or contextual variables. Branched polling narratives transform answering questions into a playful storytelling experience. This results in rich and relevant public responses, which can then inform public policy. In addition, the devices can communicate near real-time information, making it possible for passers-by to respond also to this data.

↑ 2 ↑ 3

The 3D-printed weatherproof enclosure was engineered to be modular and attachable to various forms of urban infrastructure, for example, fences, trees and bike racks. Different installation constellations, featuring one or multiple screens, can be deployed depending on need. Due to the e-paper displays, the devices can be powered by batteries, and therefore, installed at any location, regardless of direct sunlight or the availability of power infrastructure. Citizens interact with the device via large push buttons or (COVID-19-safe) foot pedals—these features act to encourage participation.

Citizen Dialog Kit has already been deployed in many cities to inform and poll citizens about local issues, collecting feedback from up to 100 citizens per day with a diverse demographic make-up. A variety of stakeholders have utilised the toolkit, from rural municipalities to cities, to regional governments and NGO's. This type of citizen engagement aims to integrate bottom-up values and preferences into decision-making to increase the quality of decisions, inform citizens, foster trust and reduce conflict.

↑ 4
← 5

142 / PRACTICE / PARTICIPATORY ARCHITECTURE AND INFRASTRUCTURES

Project Credits
Jorgos Coenen
Sandy Claes
Andrew Vande Moere
Research[x]Design—KU Leuven
Daan Wampers
OrganiCity (H2020)

Media Credits
Paul Biedermann (3)
Jorgos Coenen (1, 2, 4–6)

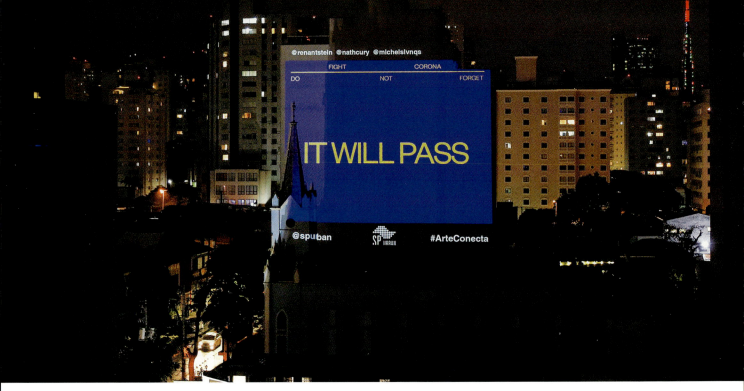

↑1 →2

SP_Urban
Arte Conecta

São Paulo, Belo Horizonte, Rio de Janeiro,
São José dos Campos; Brazil
2020

Until quarantine, windows were merely membranes that separated private space from public. But in Brazil, after a few weeks of confinement, windows became spaces of protest, of performance, and a place to socialise where possible and create community. Arte Conecta was envisioned as a creative breath of fresh air to break up the monotonous routine and open up colourful windows in the grey cities.

Media artworks from more than 50 artists were projected onto the buildings of four Brazilian cities. This collaborative project aimed to disperse information and to improve the physical and psychological wellbeing of a population in social isolation.

↑ 3 ↑ 4

The program was broadcast in a synchronised way in nine locations in São Paulo, Belo Horizonte, Rio de Janeiro and São José dos Campos. Projectors were located in the apartment windows of artists and collaborators. The artistic projections took advantage of people's gaze being directed outward from their windows and became a way to connect art, artists and the population in a safe way, respecting the rules of lockdown.

    Through online collaboration, visual artists, VJs and illustrators sent works that expressed a feeling of togetherness, empathy, gratitude and humour. A significant number of the works proclaimed messages against the violation of civil rights and the abuse of public power. Artists also reinforced social and health practices to help control COVID-19. Visuals were displayed at a standard 1080 x 1080 pixels to fit buildings of different sizes, and a variety of different projectors and lens were used.

The SP_Urban Arte Conecta festival sought to reflect on the challenges posed at this new social juncture through different perspectives. With the motto: 'It is necessary to imagine, to daydream in order to enhance the human capacity to plan possible futures', the festival made use of the communication potential of urban media and massive engagement on social networks.

↑5 ↗6

Project Credits
Marília Pasculli
Verve Cultural
Collaborative
João Frugiuele
On Projeções/ Cosmic Eventos

Media Credits
Verve Cultural (1-7)

→7

147

PRACTICE

SPATIAL
MEDIA ART

Media art is created and consumed with different intentions than those associated with the design of architecture. Projects in the category of Spatial Media Art tend to include experimental and avant-garde approaches. While at the intersection of architecture and media art, artists in this category explore aesthetics as a primary driver of their work, with architectural innovations as a secondary aspect of the projects. These projects employ a diverse range of media, including robotic kinetics, interactive light and sound, water and air, digital compositions of video and mirrored projections to celebrate, commemorate, comment on or engage with broader societal and historical issues.

Fundamental to the projects is a creative combination of digital technologies, in many cases used to include people as active participants in the artworks. The spatial and material characteristics of the built environment and the context of the projects are also critical ingredients. The artists are playful in their explorations and experiments, resulting in beautiful and highly impactful works. The installations have unique compositions of light, colour, movement and imagination to stimulate the senses and create immersive spatial experiences. While some of the chosen projects are temporary installations, others are permanently on display and well-integrated into their sites. Each installation seeks to add layers of symbolic meaning to places or activate public spaces in innovative and artistic ways.

← LEVENSLICHT, p. 162. Image courtesy of Studio Roosegaarde

Halo

London, United Kingdom
2018

In a transient moment, when wind, sun, water and technology aligned perfectly, a sculpture of sunlight appeared. This was Halo: a circle of light created by an array of 99 robotic mirrors, which move like sunflowers throughout the day to catch the sun. Each mirror reflected a line of sunlight into the mist of water, with these beams interacting to create Halo.

Halo was presented in the Edmond J. Safra Fountain Court at Somerset House. When the artists, Kimchi and Chips, visited Somerset House, they were struck by the quality and colour of the sunlight in the courtyard, as it reflected from the surrounding building, and the way in which the architecture aligned with the midday sun. This isolated volume of natural light and wind, contained within the architecture of the building, presented itself as a canvas.

Kimchi and Chip's projects explore the idea of 'drawing in the air', often using light as a medium. Halo is the first large-scale project in which the artists have worked solely with natural light and embraced the unpredictability of the weather, collaborating directly with the natural fluctuations of the climate.

To create the sculpture the artists built a heliostat array to draw lines of sunlight into an atomised mist of water. A careful balance between nature and technology had to occur, so that the formation of the circle of light was both a coincidence and an inevitability. The viewer could never know at which exact moment Halo would form, only that it eventually would appear, if they looked for long enough. At the moment that Halo emerged in the air, the transience of life and the eternal nature of the sun briefly superimposed, creating a form that exists at the boundary between the material and immaterial.

Project Credits
Kimchi and Chips
Somerset House
Studio Sungshin
Hurst Peirce + Malcolm LLP
Dynamixel
Rulr
Arts Council Korea
Arts Council England
Gwangju Design Biennale
Somerset House Trust
Korean Cultural Centre UK

Media Credits
Kimchi and Chips (1-6)

151

←3

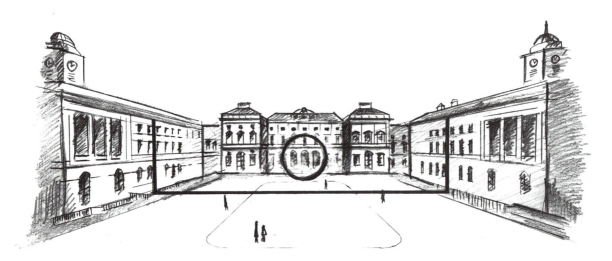

Sep. 2016
concept sketch

←4

152 / PRACTICE / SPATIAL MEDIA ART

→ 5

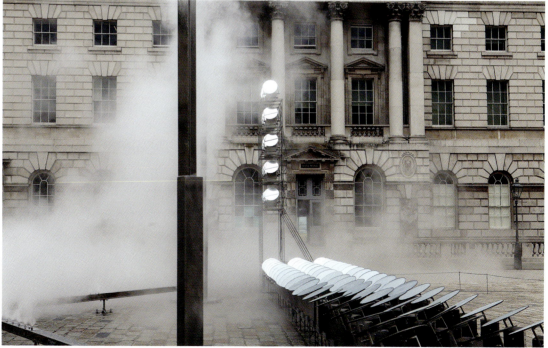
→ 6

↑1

Merck Light Cloud

Darmstadt, Germany
2018

Located in a mirrored atrium between two buildings, the Merck Light Cloud turns even short everyday walks into extraordinary sensory experiences. The sculpture consists of four curved metal strands with 576 OLED panels attached. The constantly shifting light they generate is visually multiplied by mirrors on the walls and ceiling. Sensors distributed throughout the room register the movement of visitors, allowing the installation to constantly interact with them. The result is an infinite, three-dimensional mosaic of light and sound in which visitors leave their tracks.

Constructed inside the Merck Innovation Centre in Darmstadt, the installation transforms the company's invisible processes, idea flows and innovation into a new kind of audiovisual experience. The Light Cloud consists of four three-dimensionally curved metal strands made of powder-coated steel that overlap concentrically but slightly offset. Individual 'branches' are attached to the main strands. Each branch features two OLED panels facing opposite directions, with all branches aligned identically.

↑2

Merck Light Cloud is controlled by a 3D real-time editor. Eighteen effects are possible, with combinations of two different effects available via addition, subtraction, multiplication or fade to create interesting reactions. The specific light movement, rhythm and position of the luminous clusters are potentially infinitely variable. A total of 85 scenes have been saved, many of which are interactive, and different variations are activated in daily operation.

At different times of the day, the Merck Light Cloud generates distinct moods and creates new patterns related to the physical presence of visitors. New sounds are composed generatively in reaction to a visitor's movement. Light effects change in response to specific sounds such as the frequency of an audio signal. The installation reacts to movement with light effects, for example, by following visitors with light animations as they explore the installation.

↑ 3
← 4

↑ 5

Project Credits
TAMSCHICK MEDIA+SPACE
iart
Merck Group
HENN
OLEDWorks
Kling Klang Klong

Media Credits
iart, TAMSCHICK MEDIA+SPACE (1–5)

↑1

Where Do We Go From Here?

Hull, United Kingdom
2017

In the night-time streets of Hull's Old Town, dormant robots awakened, illuminating the architecture and casting strange shadows. Where Do We Go From Here? was an exhilarating mix of art and technology that used a specially choreographed interplay of light, shadow and sound to guide people through the streets and alleyways.

Robots communicated through woven light networks, creating kinetic animations that resulted in an inquisitive relationship to the city. The effects generated by the robots, from beams and constellations of light to shadows and reflections, animated and highlighted unseen places and architectural features. The robots interacted with one another and with Hull's residents and visitors, sparking new conversations about city and possible futures. The installation was accompanied by curated soundscapes, devised by manipulating the whirrs and clicks the robots make as they move.

↑ 2

A variety of different lighting styles were used for effect. A range of end effector lights and reflectors created theatrical lighting arrangements. Moving head lights produced striking geometric formations. Fixed light blinked like Morse code to evoke the idea of robots communicating. Spot lights danced across buildings and paving stones, making it appear as if the robots were investigating the space. Lights with directional speakers created an immersive experience.

Where Do We Go From Here? focused on four areas around Hull's Old Town. This part of the city has a rich maritime heritage and a diverse combination of architectural styles. Each site featured a different configuration of repurposed industrial robots of varying sizes, from ground to rooftop. Unique choreographies portrayed narratives that posed important questions about the role of robots in society. The robots were programmed to shine a light on the historical tapestry in which they were situated—emphasising the ways in which old and new can live in symbiosis—in a city known for both its heritage and reputation for innovation.

↑ 3

Project Credits
Jason Bruges Studio
Hull 2017
Structure Workshop
The White Wall
Niccy Hallifax
Arts Council England
Spirit of 2012

Media Credits
James Medcraft, courtesy of Jason Bruges Studio (1–4)

160 / PRACTICE / SPATIAL MEDIA ART

LEVENSLICHT

Rotterdam, The Netherlands
2020

It is the Jewish custom to place stones on a grave to honour the deceased, rather than flowers. This tradition was the inspiration for LEVENSLICHT: 104,000 luminescent memorial stones arranged in a large circle to remember the 104,000 Dutch victims of the Holocaust. The monument provided a public space for contemplation about the Holocaust and the broader importance of freedom.

LEVENSLICHT—Light of Life—is a national memorial created 75 years on from the date that the international symbol of the Holocaust, the concentration and extermination camp Auschwitz, was liberated. Daan Roosegaarde and his team of designers were tasked with creating a national work to commemorate this occasion, in collaboration with the National Committee for 4 and 5 May.

↑2 →3

By using invisible ultraviolet light, the specially developed stones with fluorescent pigments can light up every few seconds, like a breath of light. LEVENSLICHT makes the scale of the tragedy tangible; the viewer is confronted with a sea of glowing, blue stones they can reach out and touch, each one representing a life lost. As Roosegaarde describes 'LEVENSLICHT is not a traditional static monument in which people are purely observers; it asks for social participation.'

The artwork was exhibited initially in Rotterdam, lighting up the banks of the river Maas. Afterwards, LEVENSLICHT was shared among 170 local municipalities with a Holocaust history in The Netherlands, raising awareness of the devastating consequences. Never before has the Holocaust been commemorated in so many places at the same time.

The horror of the Holocaust is described by survivors as 'beyond words'. Design creates a more associative interaction as a platform for sharing: for some Holocaust survivors LEVENSLICHT helps them to connect to emotional stories, which they share with their children and grandchildren. For others it is an activator—a reminder of the importance of freedom in the future.

Project Credits
Daan Roosegaarde
Studio Roosegaarde
National Committee for 4 and 5 May

Media Credits
Studio Roosegaarde (1-6)

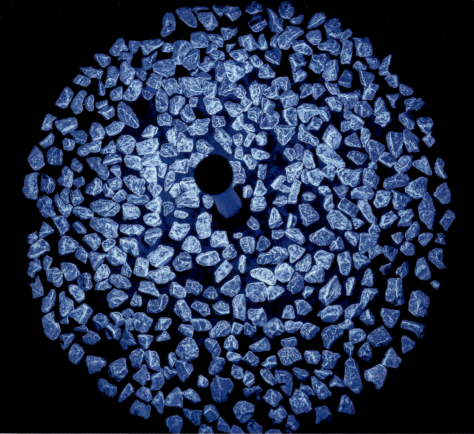

↖4 ↑5
→6

↑ 1

Variegation Index

London, United Kingdom
2019

A geometric cascade of digital 'cells' reveals invisible biological processes, in a language of oscillating light and numbers, and breathes life into a corporate lobby. Variegation Index explores the role plants have in giving feedback to their environment through photosynthesis. An array of plants is discreetly 'observed', and their photosynthetic activity is translated onto the cellular canvas.

Variegation Index is the first of Jason Bruges's work to directly involve living materials and explores the interconnectivity between technology, nature and wellbeing. The installation takes inspiration from Normalised Difference Vegetation Index (NDVI) cameras: a specialised system that farmers use to monitor the health of their crops. Chlorophyll levels within the leaves of the plants are measured

↑ 2

using a combination of infrared and RGB image capture. Energy and nutrient transfer are then displayed as a pattern of numerals and fluctuating light across the 293 digital cells of the artistic media canvas. Bright daylight is reflected as vivid, fast-moving light, which dulls and becomes slower if it is overcast or when night falls. If the artwork is viewed at an oblique angle, numerals from 1 to 9 are visible, reflecting the rate of photosynthesis observed in real time.

Bruges uses Variegation Index to explore the dichotomy between urban life and the natural world. Within the lobby of British Land's 20 Triton Street in Regent's Place, nature's rhythms are harnessed to reconnect people with the natural world and soften the existing corporate interior. Biomimicry is used in the artwork to increase the permeability between outside and inside—to disrupt the boundary between private space and public space and create a more welcoming environment.

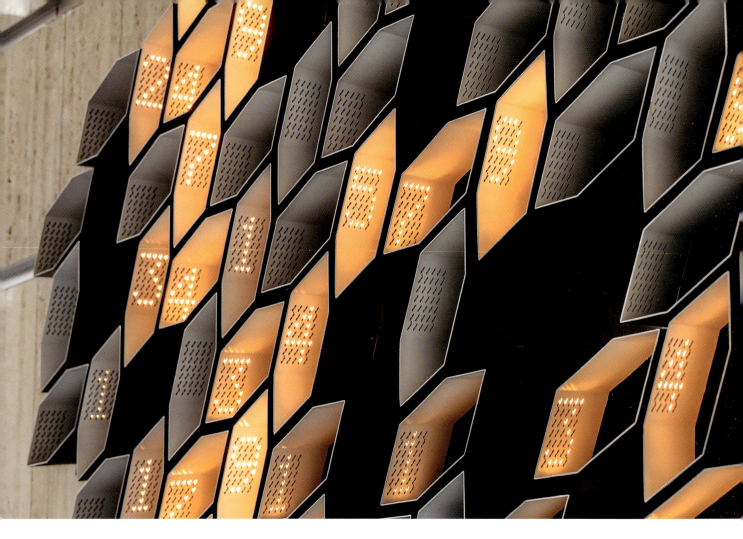

↑ 3

Project Credits
Jason Bruges Studio
British Land

Media Credits
Jason Bruges Studio (1–4)

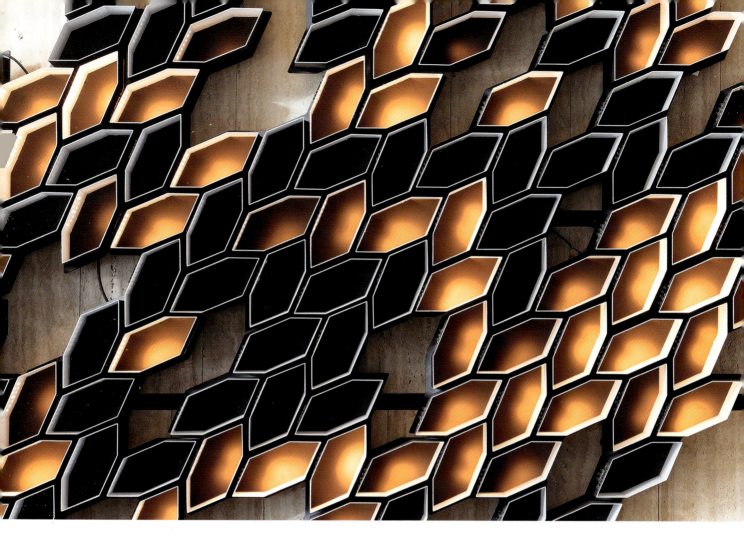

↑ 4

Wervel [Turmoil]

Groningen, The Netherlands
2019

Flowing through the centre of Forum Groningen is a force of nature made physical—a tornado hanging frozen above, its surface rippling with captured movement. Wervel [Turmoil] is an ingenious 20-metre-long, double-sided video LED sculpture. The artwork displays colourful video images of the patterns made by natural phenomena, such as turbulence and fluid dynamics, from the cosmic level to the macro and microscopic. The result is an immersive experience of light, movement and imagination that stimulates and amazes the senses.

The double-sided LED sculpture emits light through more than 1,300 flexible, thin LED panels, with over 2 million pixels. The sculpture consists of a hanging, steel structure with a complex construction of many, often double, twists. Electronics are placed inside the sculpture. Visuals display 24 hours per day and can be viewed from all angles when walking or driving around the sculpture.

170 / PRACTICE / SPATIAL MEDIA ART

→ 2

→ 3

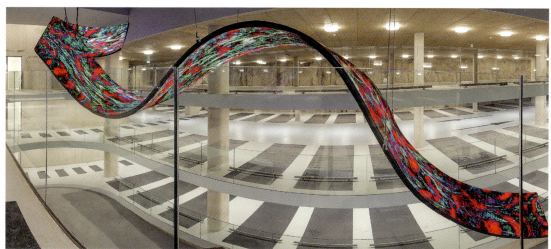

→ 4

171

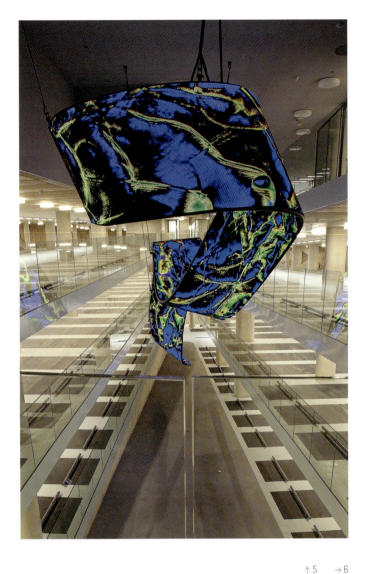

↑5 →6

Media Credits
Nicky Assmann (7)
Jenne Hoekstra (1–6)

↑ 7

Wervel [Turmoil] is saturated in intense colours achieved through video and LED light, showing nebulous forms undulating as the dynamics of viscosity and fluidity reveal mesmerising abstract images and organic visual patterns. The visuals are immersed in what Nicky Assman, the artist responsible for the work, refers to as hypercolours, which she finds both in nature and in the digital colour spectrum. The project is inspired by turbulent patterns from her previous works with liquid soap films, by fire tornadoes and by the patterns seen in solar storms and the centuries-lasting super tornadoes in the planetary atmosphere of Jupiter.

Assman used her personal database of related images and videos, collected over many years, as the input for two custom-built video synthesisers. This allowed her to compose and alter the continuously changing visuals of turbulence and fluid dynamics into 22 unique videos, which are shown in a random order.

Project Credits
Nicky Assmann
Forum Groningen
NL Architects
ABT Engineering
DOK
Spectro Productions
Joris Strijbos
Nenad Popov
Jean-Michel Couturier
Cycling '74
Dieter Vandoren
Kunstpunt Groningen
Nicoline Wijnja
Jan Samsom
Gemeente Groningen
Mondriaan Fonds

FUTURE TRENDS AND PROTOTYPES

PRACTICE

The category of Future Trends and Prototypes includes projects that reflect areas of growing attention or concern, such as climate change, carbon neutral design, artificial intelligence and machine learning. Digital and interactive technologies are becoming more accessible to novice users in both their cost and ease of use. With this shift there is increasing room for non-expert users to play, experiment with and push the boundaries of what can be done in the realm of media architecture. Future Trends and Prototypes demonstrate the latest installations and projects that continue to broaden the horizons of media architecture.

Some of the projects are large scale buildings or festivals requiring large teams of designers, artists, scientists and supporters while other projects are research driven and emerging from small teams of investigators. The projects incorporate many established media architecture design elements, including lighting displays and interactive technologies, while at the same time exhibiting a shift in the field towards the integration of new technologies, such as novel forms of artificial intelligence specific to media architecture.

While they are thought-provoking and stimulate the senses, these projects elicit new questions and inspire novel ways of seeing the world and considering our future. With a tendency to promote curiosity, play and openness, the projects create dialogues between the designers and users that remark on the current state of the world and create engaging views on future trends that are certain to lead the next generation of media architecture.

← Woodie, p. 196. Image courtesy of Destination NSW.

SMOG FREE PROJECT

Beijing, Tianjin, Dalian; China
Rotterdam, The Netherlands
Krakow, Poland
2018

Pollution has become something we accept as a normal part of our lives. The SMOG FREE PROJECT aims to combat this assumption by creating 'bubbles' of clean air for people, including students, governments and the clean-tech industry, to think, meet and work together to make the whole city smog free. A series of urban innovations led by Daan Roosegaarde—including SMOG FREE TOWER, SMOG FREE RING and SMOG FREE BICYCLE—provide local solutions to air quality in public spaces. The project follows Roosegaarde's ethos: to make people part of the solution instead of the problem.

The world's first smog vacuum cleaner, the seven-metres-tall, aluminium SMOG FREE TOWER, uses patented positive ionisation technology to create smog free air in public spaces, allowing people to breathe and experience clean air for free. It is equipped with environment-friendly technology, cleans 30,000 cubic metres per hour and uses very little, green electricity. The tower provides a local solution to air quality such as in parks. The effectiveness of SMOG FREE TOWER has been validated by the Eindhoven University of Technology.

↑ 2

SMOG FREE RING is a tangible souvenir made from smog collected from the SMOG FREE TOWER. By sharing the ring, you donate 1000 cubic metres of clean air to the city. The profit from the ring is used to develop more smog free solutions. SMOG FREE BICYCLE is an innovative bicycle that inhales polluted air, cleans it and then releases the cleaned air around the cyclist. The first prototype was inspired by manta rays—a fish that filters water for food. The intention is to make it a medium for smog free cities, with many thousands of bicycles creating an impact on a larger urban scale.

↑ 3

Project Credits
Daan Roosegaarde
Studio Roosegaarde
ENS Technology
Advisor Ursem
China Central Government
Embassy of the Kingdom of the Netherlands in China
ING Poland
Film Method Works
City of Rotterdam
Stichting Doen
Port of Rotterdam
M4H
IABR

Media Credits
Studio Roosegaarde (1–5)

↑4 →5

← 1

One Shenzen Bay

Shenzen, China
2018

It is easy to forget about nature in the middle of a busy city landscape crowded with skyscrapers. One Shenzhen Bay connects the natural world to architecture by collecting real-time data from a weather station located on its 350-metre-high roof. Wind speed and direction, air quality, tidal movements, temperature and humidity data are gathered and used to create four chapters of architectural media art using data visualisation techniques. Passers-by taking a moment to look up at a skyscraper resplendent with glittering light are reminded of the force and infinite changeability of nature.

The four chapters convey different meanings and transform One Shenzhen Bay into a pillar of shimmering light: in Chapter I 'A Roc flies over the Top Sky' real-time meteorological data is translated into visible light streams; in Chapter II 'Gorgeous clouds charm' sunset colours pulse; Chapter III 'Guide the New Journey' is a galaxy of sparkling lights; and in Chapter IV 'Voyage far and wide' light beams flow like sea waves.

Thought was given to ensuring that the exterior lighting products did not disturb residents of the building. Thin horizontal LED lighting was chosen and adapted to the architecture to conceal the lighting products from interior spaces. The horizontal light lines remain unobtrusive at close proximities but create coherent imagery when viewed at a distance.

In order to involve city dwellers further, an interactive app links users to a series of charity programs, including the ONE SHENZHEN BAY WALK PROGRAM. Each day, users can donate their steps once they reach a target number. These will be converted into a donation fund to tackle environmental problems and improve the lives of sanitation workers in poverty. Users can find their own walk tracks on the animated media architecture, which will be integrated with the app—the animation will be displayed on both building and app simultaneously.

Project and Media Credits
Lighting Stories (Beijing) Cultural & Creative Co., Ltd
ZHENG Jianwei
SHENG Yanming
LI Hao
Kohn Pedersen Fox Associated PC
Zhouwen Chen
ParkLand Real Estate Development
CCDI GROUP
Licht Kunst Licht AG
Andreas Schulz
Lucas King
Yichen Jiang
Stephan Thiele
Osram
Derivative TouchDesigner
ZENG Wanqiong
WANG Zhitao

←2

← 3

182 / PRACTICE / FUTURE TRENDS AND PROTOTYPES

← 4

↑1

Archive Dreaming

Istanbul, Turkey
2017

What would it look like if we could visualise a database's thoughts? Its dreams? Archive Dreaming was an immersive architectural experience that explored machine learning by letting you examine 1.7 million documents and display the connections between them. The installation was user-driven, but, when idle, it 'dreamed' of unexpected correlations between the documents.

Archive Dreaming was a six-metre-wide, circular installation displayed at the SALT Galata as part of *The Uses of Art: Final Exhibition*. It was created by Refik Anadol Studio in collaboration with Google's Artists and Machine Intelligence—a program exploring cutting-edge developments in the field of machine intelligence in an environment that brings together artists and engineers.

The installation employs machine learning algorithms to search and sort relationships between the documents from the 17th to 20th century Ottoman Bank's cultural archive. A neural network was trained using images of the 1.7 million documents at SALT Research. The resulting high-dimensional data and interactions were translated into an all-encompassing environment that transgressed the normal boundaries of the viewing experience of a library—the user was surrounded by a three-dimensional and architectonic visualisation of the archive.

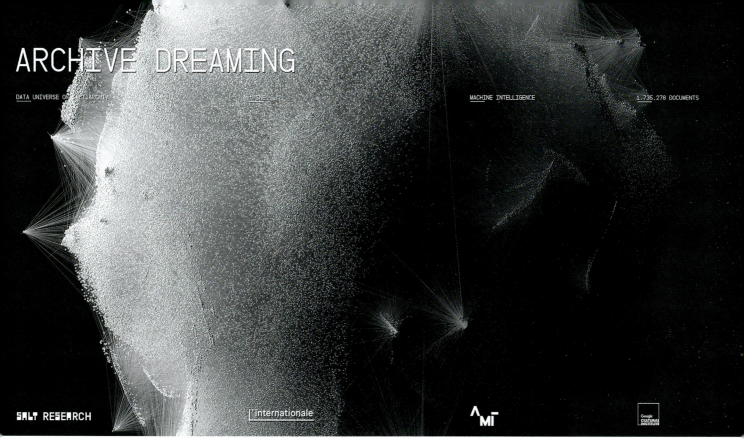

↑2 →3

Visitors entered Archive Dreaming through a corridor to find themselves in a circular room with curved projection surfaces all around them. Mirrors on the floor and ceiling completed the effect of being 'inside' the inner workings of the archive. The user could select documents to view on a tablet. Depending on the choice made, the viewer was immersed in data given form, perhaps constellations of light created from data connections or a lattice of complex clustered information.

There were 40,000 visitors to Archive Dreaming, many of them students seeking to enhance their understanding of machine learning and how it could be used to explore the previously invisible universe of an archive.

↑ 4
← 5

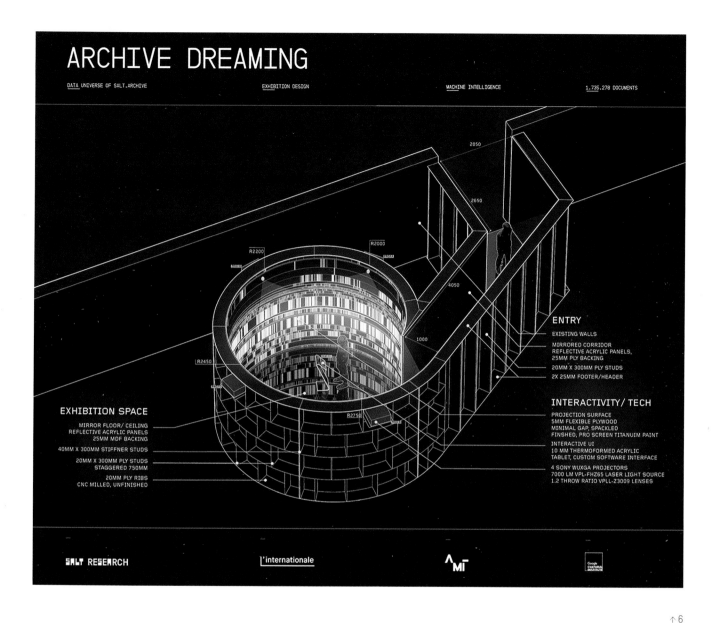

↑ 6

Project Credits
Refik Anadol
Raman K. Mustafa
SALT
Refik Anadol Studio
Google AMI

Media Credits
Refik Anadol (1-6)

↑1

Novartis Pavillon

Basel, Switzerland
2021

As the world strives for net zero, a media facade that generates its own electricity represents a unique fusion of artistic expression, science and sustainability. After dark, the Novartis Pavillon comes alive with subtle light shows created by renowned artists and powered by a network of translucent cells equipped with organic solar panels. Designed to inspire curiosity in the onlooker, the facade symbolically conveys the intention of the building—to promote dialogue and openness.

The construction consists of a net-like membrane attached to the sheet metal facade of the building. A total of 10,000 rhombus-shaped, organic solar cells are screwed into the mesh, with around 7,000 facing outward and equipped with LED modules. Using the electricity generated by the cells, the building is illuminated with direct and indirect light, depending on the time of day.

188 / PRACTICE / FUTURE TRENDS AND PROTOTYPES

↑ 2

The technology of organic photovoltaics makes it possible to create media facades that meet both aesthetic and ecological requirements. The solar cells are thin, flexible, semi-transparent and almost freely designable, which means they can be used to develop structures with a balanced or even positive energy consumption and a small CO_2 footprint. The electricity generated by the solar cells is used to illuminate Novartis Pavillon. Each outward-facing cell is equipped with bi-directional LED modules—one LED unit points away from the facade and one points onto it. The organic solar cells are translucent, so the light shines through them. During the day, the facade uses the direct light emitted by the forward-facing LEDS, while at night it is illuminated by indirect light.

The facade is able to display low-resolution scrolling text and video content. Artists have collaborated with scientists to develop light installations inspired by life science: from the shapes and colours of cells and molecules to the graphs that display climate change data.

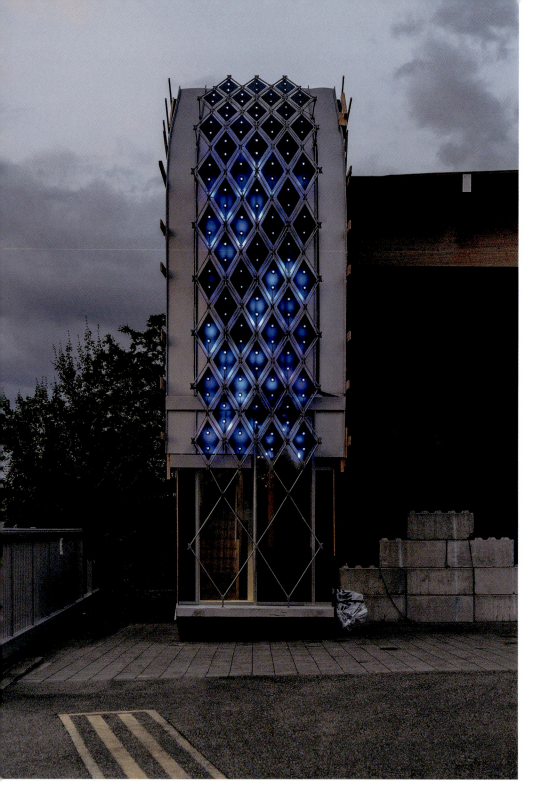

190 / PRACTICE / FUTURE TRENDS AND PROTOTYPES

Project Credits
iart
Novartis Pharma AG
AMDL CIRCLE
Blaser Architekten
formTL
TouchDesigner
ARMOR solar power films GmbH

Media Credits
iart (1–3)

↑1

Uptown Underground

New York City, United States of America
2019

Does a subway have something to learn from a glass-bottom boat? An artist sought to answer this question with Uptown Underground, an installation on a moving train deep below the streets of New York City.

On a glass-bottom boat tour, Ian Callender became fascinated with the way the vehicle transporting him had suddenly become a portal to the world below it—the movement of the reeds, the fish darting by, the darkness of the depths—providing a context he had been previously missing. A few days later, riding the subway at his home in New York, he understood that here too context was absent. The passengers on the train could move through the city without the fantastic experience of looking up and around at the buildings they were speeding past. Could it be possible to peel back the metal ceiling of the subway car and bring the city into it?

Installed without permission on the 6 Train from Brooklyn Bridge-City Hall to 96th Street, Uptown Underground was a geographically accurate view of the New York cityscape above the subway train, projected onto its ceiling. Like a glass-bottom boat flipped upside down, the moving images allowed passengers to reconnect with their urban surroundings. The installation was implemented using four projectors connected to Raspberry Pi's, synchronised with offsets over a peer-to-peer wi-fi network and informed by geolocation and acceleration data from a smartphone. This was all achieved using only battery power.

192 / PRACTICE / FUTURE TRENDS AND PROTOTYPES

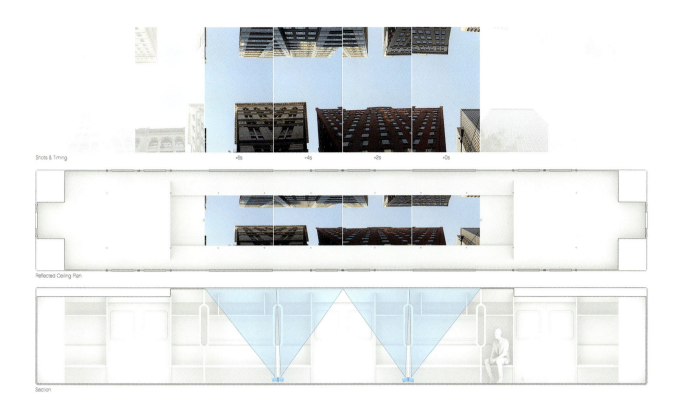

↑ 2

↑ 3

← 4

← 5

← 6

194   / PRACTICE / FUTURE TRENDS AND PROTOTYPES

←7

Project Credits
Ian Callender
New York City Metropolitan Transportation Authority
Scott Zaretsky
Daniel Ornitz
Marcus Odom
Matthew Lesko

Media Credits
Ian Callender (1–7)

Woodie

Sydney, Australia
2019

Cities around the globe are increasingly becoming testbeds for urban robotic experimentation. But these robots are mainly utilised to perform mundane tasks. What if we designed robots with the aim of facilitating more engaging creative and playful public spaces? Woodie is a slow-moving urban robot that draws on the ground using luminescent sidewalk chalk. The area in which Woodie wanders around is illuminated with ultraviolet lights, turning the surrounding public space into a large horizontal canvas made of glowing words and drawings.

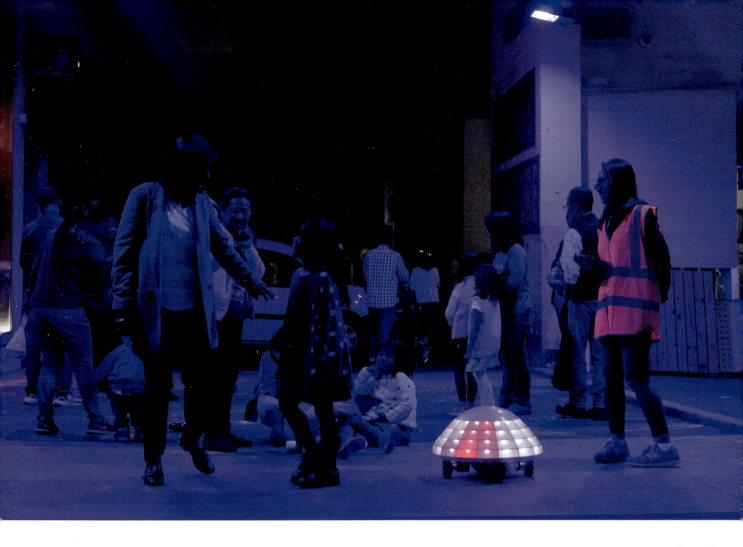

↖1 ↑2

Woodie was a temporary installation designed by Marius Hoggenmüller, Luke Hespanhol and Martin Tomitsch and deployed in a quiet laneway in Chatswood for Vivid Sydney: a festival of light, music and ideas. Passers-by were attracted to Woodie's luminous shell, which has a low-resolution lighting display integrated into it. They were enticed to stop and contemplate the robot, and finally join in and draw with it and other people. Research has shown that conventional public displays in cities are often ignored by people due to the oversaturation of digital screens in our lives. Woodie instead combines hi-tech and futuristic design with a low-tech and traditional form of urban storytelling—chalk drawings on the street.

↑ 3

Capable of translating digital illustrations into simple line drawings, Woodie can communicate with passers-by to let them know about its creative process, the direction it intends to move or to cheekily complain if someone blocks its path. To allow people to add their own drawings, luminescent chalk sticks were made available around the installation site. Woodie successfully attracted people's attention—provoking emotional responses where people behaved as though it were a living being—and acted as a facilitator for collaborative, creative placemaking. Instead of striving for ever-increasing productivity and efficiency in cities, the installation explores the potential for robots to trigger urban reflection and encourage taking a moment to slow down.

198 / PRACTICE / FUTURE TRENDS AND PROTOTYPES

↑ 4

Project Credits
Marius Hoggenmüller
Luke Hespanhol
Martin Tomitsch
Design Lab, The University of Sydney
ArtNet DMX
Willoughby City Council

Media Credits
Destination NSW (1, 4)
Marius Hoggenmüller (2, 3)

Authors

Joel Fredericks is a Lecturer in Design at The University of Sydney, Director of the Bachelor of Design (Interaction Design), urban planner, community engagement practitioner and researcher. His research is transdisciplinary and sits across the domains of media architecture, smart cities, and community engagement.

Glenda Amayo Caldwell is an Associate Professor in Architecture at the the School of Architecture and Built Environment, Faculty of Engineering at the Queensland University of Technology (QUT) in Brisbane, Australia. She is an architecture and design scholar, leading Industry 4.0 innovation through human-centred research in design robotics, media architecture, and Human-Building Interaction.

Martin Tomitsch is a Professor and Head of the Transdisciplinary School at the University of Technology Sydney, a founding member of the Media Architecture Institute and the Life-centred Design Collective, author of "Making Cities Smarter" and lead author "Design Think Make Break Repeat".

M. Hank Haeusler is an Associate Professor at The University of New South Wales, Director of Computational Design, Director of the ARC Centre for Next-Gen Architectural Manufacturing, Deputy Director UNSW AI Institute, Head of Research, Foresight and Innovation at Giraffe Technology, and known as researcher, educator, and entrepreneur in media architecture and computational design through over 140 publications.

Dave Colangelo is Assistant Professor at The Creative School, Toronto Metropolitan University and Director, Media Architecture Institute, North America. Dave is also a founding member of Public Visualization Studio. His work examines urban media environments as sites for critical and creative engagements with the city, public art, and information.

Martijn de Waal is a professor in Civic Interaction Design at the Amsterdam University of Applied Sciences. In 2020/21 he was the general chair of the Media Architecture Biennale 2020 that took place in Amsterdam, Utrecht and online.

Ava Fatah gen. Schieck is Associate Professor, the director of Architectural Space and Computation PhD Programme, tutor for Architectural Computation at the Bartlett, UCL (UK), leading the creation and investigation of media architecture and human building interaction in living lab settings through spatial urban prototyping with local communities. Ava was the MAB conference and programme chair (2012-21).

Marcus Foth is a Professor of Urban Informatics at QUT leading interaction design research into digital media, smart cities and media architecture. Marcus founded the Urban Informatics Research Lab in 2006. He is a Fellow of the Australian Computer Society and the Queensland Academy of Arts and Sciences and a Distinguished Member of the ACM.

Luke Hespanhol is a Senior Lecturer in Design at The University of Sydney, Director of the Master of Interaction Design and Electronic Arts, artist, designer and researcher. His practice investigates the intersection of culture and technologies, through academic research, teaching, and collaborations with galleries, local government, and public art festivals.

Marius Hoggenmüller is a Lecturer in Interaction Design at the University of Sydney and co-founder of the Urban Interfaces Lab. He received his PhD from the University of Sydney, investigating the design of urban robotic interfaces. Marius has been an active researcher in the media architecture community since 2014.

Gernot Tscherteu is co-founder of the Media Architecture Institute and the Media Architecture Biennale Festival. His main interest lies in urban commons and digital tools for the self-organisation of resource communities in the domains of housing, mobility, food, and energy. He supports co-housing- and carsharing projects and energy communities at Gemeinschaffen.

Contributors

Kavita Gonsalves combines art, design, communities, technology and participatory processes to creatively and collaboratively produce guerrilla placemaking projects: Multicoloured Dreams (FIN), the Bake Collective (IND) and TransHuman Saunter (AUS). Her PhD "Radical Placemaking" focuses on the use of emerging technologies as tools for marginalized communities to engage in creative placemaking towards social justice.

Elise Hodson is a Senior Tutor in the School of Design at the Royal College of Art (London) with a background in design history and culture. As a Post-doctoral Researcher at Aalto University (Finland), she worked with colleagues to examine social value and impacts of design, particularly in smart cities.

Yu Kao is an interaction designer and researcher. She has completed her PhD in interaction design for public spaces. She is passionate about exploring novel design methods and practices to facilitate inclusive and empathetic approaches to design. Her work has been influenced by participatory design and the concept of place.

Michiel de Lange is an Assistant Professor in the Department of Media and Culture Studies at Utrecht University. His research interest concern the intersections between digital media and urban culture. He is the co-founder of The Mobile City and the [urban interfaces] research group.

Wen-Ying (Rei) Lee obtained her Ph.D. in Mechanical and Aerospace Engineering Department at Cornell University. She adopts Research through Design approaches to explore Human-Robot Interaction that is not solely driven by utilitarian values. Her thesis work proposes a character-driven robot design approach as an alternative to design social robots.

Jock McQueenie is a QUT Industry Fellow who has pioneered the 3C project design methodology that brings together Community, Culture and Commerce. He has been designing and implementing 3C projects for 20+ years. Adding value to corporate social investment, Jock's intermediary practice brokers unconventional partnerships for mutual benefit. His work was recognised with an Australian Good Design Award 2020.

Michel Nader is a designer, MA from Aalto University, interested in how societies interact with and are affected by design. His experience is in social impact of design, change in social systems and inclusivity in the design process. He enjoys collaborative projects, teamwork, creative methods and audiovisual methods for ethnographic research.

Teija Vainio Ph.D. (information technology) has also studied architecture and art history. Currently she teaches at the Department of Design at Aalto University, Finland. Her research addresses two broad topics: human-technology interaction and experience design. Her current work focuses on the experience design methods and experience design in urban environments.

Alexander Wiethoff is a lecturer at the University of Munich and design manager at IMAGO Design GmbH, a design agency that develops products for the medical industry. He has a background in electrical engineering, architecture, UX design, and contemporary art. He enjoys conducting field studies, teaching at universities, and prototyping.

Imprint

Publication Leads
Joel Fredericks, Glenda Amayo Caldwell, Martin Tomitsch and M. Hank Haeusler

Concept and Implementation
Joel Fredericks and Martin Tomitsch

Copy Editing
Verity Borthwick

Layout and Graphic Design
Ryan Phung and Sean Akahane-Bryen

Concepts and Methods Sections
Texts by: Glenda Amayo Caldwell, Dave Colangelo, Michiel de Lange, Martijn de Waal, Ava Fatah gen. Schieck, Marcus Foth, Joel Fredericks, Kavita Gonsalves, M. Hank Haeusler, Luke Hespanhol, Elise Hodson, Marius Hoggenmüller, Yu Kao, Wen-Ying Lee, Jock McQueenie, Michel Nader Sayún, Martin Tomitsch, Gernot Tscherteu, Teija Vainio, Alexander Wiethoff

Practice Section
Media Architecture Biennale Awards 2018 and 2020
Texts sourced and edited by Verity Borthwick. Images based on submissions made to the Media Architecture Biennale Awards 2018 and 2020, image credits are listed for each project in alphabetical order.

Publication Funding
Amsterdam University of Applied Sciences
Queensland University of Technology
The University of New South Wales
The University of Sydney

Companion Website
https://mac2.mediaarchitecture.org

Cover Photo
Daan Roosegaarde
Studio Roosegaarde
www.studioroosegaarde.net

Production
avedition GmbH, Stuttgart
Publishers for Architecture and Design

© Copyrights 2023 avedition GmbH, Stuttgart
Publishers for Architecture and Design

© Copyrights for texts and photos with individual authors, companies and photographers

This work is subject to copyrights. All rights are reserved, whether the whole or part of the materials is concerned, and specifically but not exclusively the rights of translation, reprinting, reuse of illustrations, recitations, broadcasting, reproduction on microfilms or in other ways, and storage in data banks or any other media. For use of any copyrights owner must be obtained.

ISBN: 978-3-89986-393-2
Printed in Europe

avedition GmbH Senefelderstr. 109
70176 Stuttgart Germany
contact@avedition.com
www.avedition.com